W9-DBU-630

# DR. DAVID JEREMIAH

# Ten Questions Christians are Asking

Let God Turn Your
Question Marks Into
Exclamation Points

© 2015 Turning Point for God
P.O. Box 3838
San Diego, CA 92163
All Rights Reserved

Edited by Robert J. Morgan

Unless otherwise indicated, Scripture verses quoted are from
the NEW KING JAMES VERSION.

Printed in the United States of America.

# Table of Contents

# Introduction

————○————

When President Ronald Reagan addressed the Gridiron Club at the Capital Hilton Hotel in Washington, D.C., on March 26, 1988, he opened with one of his inimitable quips. "Before I refuse to take your questions," he said, "I have an opening statement."[1]

The crowd gave him a hearty laugh, but there was truth in what he said. Most politicians would rather make statements than answer questions. So would most preachers. So would most of us. It's easy to make statements, state opinions, preach sermons, give advice, declare truth, and tell others what we think. Often we should, for the Bible tells us to speak the truth in love. We have a Gospel to proclaim and a testimony to bear. Jesus made many statements; yet much of His ministry was spent asking and answering questions.

He started early. The second chapter of Luke's Gospel gives us the one and only extant scene from our Lord's childhood, when at age twelve He stayed behind in Jerusalem while His parents traveled home thinking He was in the company of their group. It took seventy-two anxious hours for Joseph and Mary to double back and locate Him. They finally found their Son ensconced in the Temple, engaged in question-and-answer sessions with the rabbis.

Luke wrote, "After three days they found Him in the temple, sitting in the midst of the teachers, both listening to them and asking them questions. And all who heard Him were astonished at His understanding and answers" (Luke 2:46-47).

Notice that He was asking questions and He was also giving answers.

In the next verse, the Lord's exasperated mother had a question of her own. "Son," asked Mary, "why have You done this to us?"

The twelve-year-old didn't just answer her question with a question, but with two of them: "Why did you seek Me? Did you not know that I must be about My Father's business?"

That was the beginning of a ministry of questions. When you read the four Gospels looking for question marks, you'll find them everywhere. Jesus knew all the answers, yet He was endlessly asking and answering questions. By studying our Lord's use of questions, we see how His wisdom intersected with human need.

*What do you want Me to do for you? Who do men say that I, the Son of Man, am? Who do you say that I am? Who is My mother and who are My brothers? Why do you think evil in your hearts? Do you love Me more than these? Who touched Me? What will it profit a man if he gains the whole world, and loses his own soul? Of how much more value are you than the birds? Why are you anxious? Woman, why are you weeping? Whom are you seeking? How many loaves do you have? Were there not ten cleansed? Where are the nine? Do you believe that I am able to do this? Why make this commotion and weep? Why do you call Me "Lord, Lord," and not do the things which I say? Will you lay down your life for My sake? Could you not watch with Me one hour? What kind of conversation is this that you have with one another as you walk and are sad? Shall I not drink the cup which My Father has given Me? My God, My God, why have You forsaken Me?[2]*

From the casual to the crucial, Jesus used the grappling hooks of questions to snag His hearers' interest, grasp their thoughts, reveal their motives, explore their needs, and clench their decisions.

If the Lord Jesus came to speak one Sunday at my church, I wonder what questions He would ask and what questions He would answer. I'd want to be first in line with my list. I know what it's like to have poignant questions deep down in my soul. Some questions are so painful, we're afraid to ask them. Other questions are so helpful, the answers can bless all the world.

Much of my life has been seeking out answers for life from the Word of God, first to satisfy my own mind and heart, and then to meet the needs of others. Throughout my years of ministry, I have found I feel closest to people's needs when I'm dealing with their most heartfelt questions. Yes, I love to make statements and preach sermons; but I never want to disregard those sincere questions that embody our search for meaning. Questions are the inquiries of curious minds and the entreaties of wondering souls. Where there are question marks in our minds and spirits, we need the truths and promises of Scripture.

In that spirit, I recently asked those who attend our congregation, Shadow Mountain Community Church in San Diego, to send me questions they would ask me if we were sitting down in a coffee shop. What's on your mind? What's on your heart? What perplexes you? What troubles you? What answers do you need to be a happier and stronger person?

The letters and emails came in, and I went through them carefully and selected several questions to answer in a series of Sunday morning sermons. These are the questions that appeared in my inbox over and over.

Out of those messages has come this book. I pray that as you study its pages, you'll find the answers God provides for the questions you are asking, like . . .

How Can I Be Sure of My Salvation?
How Can I Overcome Temptation?

How Can I Get Victory Over Worry?
How Can I Find Forgiveness?
Is There Only One Way to God?
Why Do Christians Have So Many Problems?
Why Don't My Prayers Get Answered?
Is There a Sin God Cannot Forgive?
What Is Faith?
What Is the Greatest Commandment?

Francis Bacon said, "A prudent question is one half of wisdom."[3] May the following pages provide the other half as we open our hearts to the answers of God's Word to the questions people are asking. I'm convinced the words of Scripture can answer the deepest needs of your life so you can say with the psalmist: "I will praise You, for You have answered me, and have become my salvation" (Psalm 118:21).

God has answers to the questions Christians are asking.

He has answers for you, and His omnipotent hand can bend your most stubborn question marks into exclamation points of praise.

———————o———————

# CHAPTER ONE

# How Can I Be Sure of My Salvation?

DO YOU KNOW WHERE YOU'RE GOING? Are you sure?

Dr. Albert Einstein, the German-born theoretical physicist who developed the theory of relativity, was well liked in his New Jersey university community. His friends, knowing of his legendary absentmindedness, looked after him. There's a tale—I don't know if it's true or apocryphal—that one day Einstein was traveling from Princeton by train. The conductor strolled down the aisle, punching the tickets of each passenger. Coming to Einstein, he waited as the great physicist reached in his vest pocket looking for his ticket. It wasn't there. He reached in his other pocket, but it wasn't there either. Einstein looked in his briefcase but couldn't find it. He looked in the seat by him but couldn't find it. The conductor said, "Dr. Einstein, I know who you are. We all know who you are. I'm sure you bought a ticket. Don't worry about it."

Einstein nodded appreciatively and the conductor continued down the aisle punching tickets. As he was ready to move to the next car, he turned around and saw the scientist down on his hands and knees looking under his seat for his ticket. The conductor rushed back and said, "Dr. Einstein, Dr. Einstein, don't worry. I know who you are. You don't need a ticket. I'm sure you bought one."

Peering up at him, Einstein said, "Young man, I too know who I am. What I don't know is where I'm going."[1]

Many people, whatever their IQs, are Einsteins today, for they don't know where they're going. Among those who wrote me, some of the most frequently asked questions were: "Am I going to heaven? How can I know? Is there any way to be sure I'm really a Christian? Can I know for certain that when I die, I'll be with the Lord? Can we be assured?"

To my amazement, most who asked these questions were church going people. Many have been in the church all their lives. Some have had a faith experience when they were small children, but over the years doubts have crept into their hearts and they have begun questioning the reality of their salvation. Bill Bright, founder of Campus Crusade for Christ (now Cru), observed, "My experience in counseling thousands of students and laymen through the years since I met Christ personally has convinced me that there are literally tens of thousands of good, faithful church-goers who have received Christ in prayer, but who are not sure of their salvation."[2]

Perhaps during their Christian experience, they've allowed some sin to take root in their lives and now they doubt if they were ever saved in the first place. Some have gotten away from a close relationship with God. Others experience doubts while going through difficult periods of life. When our bodies are sick, sometimes our souls catch the disease. It's easy to become disillusioned when our dreams are dashed, our families or our finances are in crisis, or our spirits are low.

Do you ever feel that way?

Sometimes when I've counseled those with doubts, I can trace their lack of assurance to a false teaching they've heard on the radio or on television or from a friend. Others question their salvation because they're not sure they prayed the right prayer at the time of their conversion. Many Christians are saved in childhood, but they can't remember the exact date or occasion. As a result, a nagging sense of insecurity haunts them. If you ask them if they're going to heaven, their answer will likely be something like, "I certainly hope so."

My friend Tony Evans observes, "A great spiritual malady permeates the church of Jesus Christ today. If I were to give it a name, I would call it ADD: Assurance Deficit Disorder."[3]

When you have ADD, it is almost impossible to live the Christian life as vigorously as you should. You have a difficult time praying. You seldom witness. If you aren't sure of your own salvation, why would you want to share it with anyone else? Sermons make you feel worse, not better. Worship makes you feel empty. The peace of God, so richly promised in the Bible, doesn't seem at home in your heart.

Well, I want to tell you as plainly as I can that you can know you are saved, for sure, for eternity; you can have security. You can have absolute confidence in your eternal hope. The Bible tells us we can be certain of our relationship with God and of our heavenly home. We can be persuaded. We can live beyond the needling torment of doubt. Assurance of salvation is not only possible, it is what God longs for us to possess in our minds and hearts. He does not want His children to live in insecurity, uncertainty, or uneasiness about His love for us or His ability to keep us to the end.

Donald Whitney wrote in his book on the assurance of salvation: If a governor pardons a death-row criminal, he will tell him. He will not force the condemned man to wait until his neck is in the noose to inform him he is pardoned. Likewise, when God pardons us and adopts us into His family, He does not want to hide our new status from us until the moment we stand quivering before Him, wondering if a trapdoor over hell is about to open beneath our feet. He wants us to know we're pardoned."[4]

If a human governor reassures pardoned prisoners behind bars, don't you think the Lord can reassure His pardoned children? Yes! We can be persuaded. Listen to the words of the apostle Paul in Romans 8: "For I am persuaded that neither death nor life, nor angels nor principalities nor powers, nor things present nor things to come, nor height nor depth, nor any other created thing, shall be able to separate us from the love of God which is in Christ Jesus our Lord" (verses 38-39).

Later, near the end of his life, the apostle Paul used the word *persuaded* again when he wrote, "For this reason I also suffer these things; nevertheless I am not ashamed, for I know whom I have believed and am persuaded that He is able to keep what I have committed to Him until that Day" (2 Timothy 1:12).

We can be persuaded that nothing can separate us from God, His love, and His heaven. We can be persuaded He is able to keep what we have committed to Him against that Day. We can know *what* we believe, for we can know *Whom* we have believed.

The words *assure, assuredly,* and *assurance* are basic terms in the New Testament's vocabulary.

- *Jesus said to [the thief on the cross], "**Assuredly,** I say to you, today you will be with Me in Paradise."*—Luke 23:43

- *Most **assuredly**, I say to you, he who hears My word and believes in Him who sent Me has everlasting life, and shall not come into judgment, but has passed from death into life.*—John 5:24

- *Most **assuredly**, I say to you, he who believes in Me has everlasting life.*—John 6:47

- *For our gospel did not come to you in word only, but also in power, and in the Holy Spirit and in much **assurance**.*—1 Thessalonians 1:5

- *Continue in the things which you have learned and been **assured** of.*—2 Timothy 3:14

- *We desire that each one of you show the same diligence to the full **assurance** of hope until the end.*—Hebrews 6:11

- *Let us draw near with a true heart in full **assurance** of faith.*—Hebrews 10:22

- *By this we know that we are of the truth, and shall **assure** our hearts before Him.*—1 John 3:19

The Bible uses terms like *persuaded, assurance,* and *knowing,* so I'm certain we can be persuaded, we can have assurance, and we can know for sure. Someone put it this way: "God wants us to have a 'know-so' salvation. Figuratively speaking, He does not want you to be a question mark, all bent over in doubt with your head hung low. Rather, He wants you to be an exclamation mark, standing erect with head held high, strengthened by a God-produced confidence in your faith in Him."[5]

While the entire Bible stresses certainty and assurance, there's one section of Scripture that stakes out this theme as its central focus—the letter of 1 John. It was penned by the apostle John, who wrote five New Testament books: the Fourth Gospel, the book of Revelation, and three letters, which we call 1 John, 2 John, and 3 John.

The Gospel of John and the letter of 1 John both end with similar statements, giving their respective thesis statements or declarations of purpose. Take a moment to compare these two statements carefully:

- The Gospel of John was written "that you may believe that Jesus is the Christ, the Son of God, and that believing you may have life in His name" (John 20:31).

- The book of 1 John ends by saying: "These things I have written to you who believe in the name of the Son of God, that you may know that you have eternal life . . ." (1 John 5:13).

Notice the subtle difference? The Gospel of John was written so we can believe and have life. The letter of 1 John was written that those of us who believe can *know* we have eternal life. The key word is *know*. John didn't say, "These things I have written to you who believe in the name of the Son of God, that you may hope, guess, speculate, or wish you had eternal life." There are no *ifs*, *what ifs*, *maybes*, *ands*, or *buts* to our salvation. As Steven Lawson wrote, "The greatest thing in all the world is to be saved. The second is closely related. It is to be absolutely sure that you are saved."[6]

Apparently there were some in John's day who read his Gospel and trusted Christ as their Savior, but they still harbored lingering

> *"The blood makes us safe; the Book makes us sure."*
> ~ AUTHOR UNKNOWN

doubts about their eternal destination. Like Einstein, they weren't sure where they were going. That's one of the reasons John wrote his first epistle, 1 John, to show those who had believed in Christ that they could know they were saved.

As we carefully read through 1 John, we notice a five-fold argument for the assurance of salvation. Five times in 1 John we come across the phrases "born of God" and "begotten of God." On each of these occasions, we have a different piece of evidence to reassure us of our hope. Every time John used a phrase about the new birth, he gave us another test to prove our salvation. These are five of the birthmarks of the Christian.

## The Birthmark of Confession
*1 John 5:1*

The first is the birthmark of confession, described in 1 John 5:1: "Whoever believes that Jesus is the Christ is born of God." Before you can have assurance of salvation, you have to believe and be saved. You have to confess Jesus Christ as Lord. It's possible to have a false assurance of salvation. Some people assume they are saved because they grew up in a Christian culture, or they have gone to church all their lives, or they have been baptized, or they have tried to live a good life. Yet they've never distinctly and personally confessed Jesus Christ as their Savior and Lord.

The Bible teaches that we are sinners, separated from God by a sinful nature. We can never earn, buy, or climb our way into heaven. By our own efforts or goodness, we can never be saved. That's why God became a man who lived a wholly righteous life, died on the cross, shed His blood for us, and rose from the dead. He paid our penalty, took our judgment upon Himself, and He offers us the opportunity to be born again.

In John 3, Jesus said to Nicodemus, "You must be born again" (John 3:7).

We are born again when we repent of our sins, trust Jesus Christ to save us, and confess Him as Lord of our lives. Romans 10:9 says, "If you confess with your mouth the Lord Jesus and believe in your heart that God has raised Him from the dead, you will be saved."

Notice that the verse doesn't say *you might be saved*, or *hopefully you'll be saved*, or *perhaps you'll be saved*. It says emphatically, *you will be saved*. We are saved by God's grace

> *"Examine yourselves as to whether you are in the faith. Test yourselves.."*
>
> 2 CORINTHIANS 13:5

through faith; it's not of our good works but of Christ's eternal work on the cross. Jesus said in John 5:24, "Most assuredly, I say to you, he who hears My word and believes in Him who sent Me has everlasting life, and shall not come into judgment, but has passed from death into life."

If you don't believe that Jesus Christ is God and that He is the promised Messiah and the Savior, you have not been born again. It isn't necessary to understand everything involved in these biblical truths; you have the remainder of your life to grow in grace and knowledge. But the starting point is trusting Christ as your Savior, in simple faith, believing.

In today's culture many claim to be Christians who do not truly believe Jesus is Lord. The same was true in John's day. "Beloved," he wrote in 1 John 4:1-3, "do not believe every spirit, but test the spirits, whether they are of God; because many false prophets have gone out into the world. By this you know the Spirit of God: Every spirit that confesses that Jesus Christ has come in the flesh is of God, and every spirit that does not confess that Jesus Christ has come in the flesh is not of God."

John 3:36 adds, "He who believes in the Son has everlasting life; and he who does not believe the Son shall not see life, but the wrath of God abides on him."

If someone were to ask you how you know you're a Christian, you can answer in one of two ways. If your answer begins with "Because I . . ." and proceeds to outline all that you have done to be a Christian, then you have not been born again. But if your answer begins with "Because He . . ." meaning Christ, and then you go on to describe all that Jesus has done for you, you have evidenced the first birthmark of a believer.

Now, we may not always "feel" saved even after we are saved. Sometimes we feel low in spirits, or guilty, or weary. We don't always have a strong, visceral sense of God's presence. But our assurance of salvation doesn't depend on how we feel but on what God has done and what God has said.

Additionally we have the witness of the Holy Spirit in our hearts. Romans 8:16 says, "The Spirit Himself bears witness with our spirit that we are children of God." If you have the Holy Spirit living within you, that Spirit testifies with your spirit that you are a child of God. It is the inward witness of your faith. Assurance is not about us; it is about God. How wonderful simply to trust in the finished work of Christ. How wonderful to rest in His everlasting arms.

There's an old story of a house that caught fire one night. A young boy was forced to flee to the roof. The father stood on the ground below with outstretched arms, calling to his son, "Jump! I'll catch you." He knew the boy had to jump to save his life. All the boy could see, however, were the flames, smoke, and blackness. His father kept yelling: "Jump! I will catch you." But the boy protested, "Daddy, I can't see you."

The father replied, "But I can see you and that's all that matters."

Charles Spurgeon once preached, "It is not the strength of your faith that saves you, but the strength of Him upon whom you rely. Christ is able to save you if you come to Him, be your faith weak or be it strong."

Wilbur Chapman's example provides a great case study of this. Chapman grew up in a Christian family and never knew when, where, or how he became a Christian. He does remember that his Methodist Sunday school teacher encouraged him to stand up one day and make a public declaration of faith in Christ. As a young man, he attended Oberlin College and then transferred to Lake Forest College. While he was a college student, evangelist D. L. Moody held a series of evangelistic meetings in Chicago, and many of the Lake Forest students attended, Chapman among them. They heard Moody preach, and Chapman began doubting whether or not he was really saved. He had no certainty of his salvation. At the end of the service he went into the inquiry room with others seeking spiritual counsel. To his surprise, Mr. Moody himself came in, walked over, and sat down right beside him. Chapman confessed to him that he wasn't sure whether or not he was really saved. Moody opened his Bible to John 5:24 and asked the young man to read the verse aloud. With trembling voice, Chapman read, "Verily, verily, I say unto you, He that heareth my word, and believeth on Him that sent me, hath everlasting life, and shall not come into condemnation; but is passed from death unto life" (KJV).

Moody said, "Do you believe this?"

"Certainly," said Chapman.

Moody said, "Are you a Christian?"

Chapman said, "Sometimes I think I am and again I am fearful."

"Read it again," said Moody.

Chapman read it again, and Moody repeated his two questions—Do you believe this? Are you a Christian? Chapman replied in the same way.

The great evangelist seemed a little irritated and said sharply, "Whom are you doubting?" And then he said, "Read it again."

Chapman read it again: "Verily, verily, I say unto you, He that heareth my word and believeth on Him that sent me, hath everlasting life, and shall not come into condemnation; but is passed from death unto life."

For the third time, Moody asked, "Do you believe it?"

Chapman said, "Yes, indeed I do."

"Well, are you a Christian?"

This time Chapman said, "Yes, Mr. Moody, I am."

"From that day to this," Chapman said later as a world-famed evangelist, "I have never questioned my acceptance with God."[7]

In *Simple: The Christian Life Doesn't Have to Be Complicated*, Robert J. Morgan writes: "Some people are bothered because they don't know exactly when and where they were born again; but though you may not remember the particulars, God does. It's not a question of what we remember, but of what God has done and of what God has told us in His Word. Acts 16:31 says: 'Believe on the Lord Jesus Christ, and you *will be* saved' (emphasis mine). There's no 'maybe' or 'might be' about it. The Bible uses the vocabulary of certainty. If you are actively trusting Christ right now as your Savior, there had to be a point in your past—perhaps in your childhood—when you began. Thank God for it, and don't anguish if you can't remember the exact time or place."[8]

## The Birthmark of Change
### *1 John 2:29*

If the first birthmark is our confession of Christ as our Savior and Lord, the second is a changed life, as we see in 1 John 2:29: "Everyone who practices righteousness is born of Him." When Jesus truly saves us, it makes a difference in how we think, act, speak, and conduct ourselves. The Bible says, "If anyone *is* in Christ, *he is* a new creation; old things have passed away; behold, all things have become new" (2 Corinthians 5:17).

As we begin learning to practice righteousness, our habits change. Sometimes the changes are dramatic. Some years ago, for example, a boy named Jimmy grew up on an Indiana farm. When he was a teenager, a local farmhand introduced him to the sordid world of drugs. Jimmy became instantly addicted. Within a few years he moved to Chicago and lived in holes beneath the streets where he feasted on an endless supply of heroin, opium, cocaine, and morphine. His nickname was "Jimmy the Rat."

One day, lying in a filthy bunk, Jimmy heard someone singing hymns on the street above. He recalled the songs he'd sung in church as a boy and something stirred in him. Shortly afterward, he staggered into the Pacific Garden Mission, where he heard more singing as he entered the room. Holding up both hands, he called out, "I want somebody to pray for me!"

Mission workers gathered around and earnestly prayed as he gave his life to the Lord. Jimmy's life was changed forever. By God's grace he was able to overcome his addictions. He returned to Indiana and became a successful farmer with a Christian wife and children. He often shared his testimony of God's saving grace, and his children were heard to say in their family prayers, "Thank God for Pacific Garden Mission where daddy learned to know Jesus."[9]

Every Christian has a unique testimony. Yours may not seem as dramatic as Jimmy the Rat's, but it's just as real and just as glorious, and the change should be just as lasting. We will not be sinlessly perfect while we're on this planet; but if we're Christians, we need to behave like Christians. If we say we're saved but nothing has changed about us, something is wrong. We are not saved *by* good works, but we are saved *for* good works, and the Gospel is a transforming agent in our lives.

In his epistle, John was saying, "Do you want to be sure that you have been born again? Take the belief test—what do you believe? And take the behavior test—has your life changed as the result of your belief?"

## The Birthmark of Compassion
### 1 John 4:7

Those who are truly saved also bear the birthmark of compassion. How can you know that you are a Christian? By what you believe, by how you live, and by whom you love. Love is a recurring theme in 1 John, and the apostle leaves no doubt about how it permeates the lives of true Christians. "Beloved," he wrote, "let us love one another, for love is of God; and everyone who loves is born of God and knows God. . . . We know that we have passed from death to life, because we love the brethren" (1 John 4:7; 3:14).

How do we know we are saved? By our love for our brothers and sisters in Christ.

"According to Tertullian, a prolific author and philosopher writing in the third century, the early Christian church was recognized for 'the deeds of a love so noble that lead many to put a brand upon us. See, they say, how they love one another . . . and are ready even to die for one another.' A popular hymn suggests the same sentiment: 'They will know we are Christians by our love.'"[10]

The epistle of 1 John contains some of the richest words ever written about love. The word *love* occurs 26 times in this little letter, as we read verses like, "He who loves his brother abides in the light. . . . Behold what manner of love the Father has bestowed on us, that we should be called children of God! . . . For this is the message that you heard from the beginning, that we should love one another. . . . He who does not love *his* brother abides in death. . . . By this we know love, because He laid down His life for us. . . . Whoever has this world's goods and sees his brother in need, and shuts up his heart from him, how does the love of God abide in him? My little children, let us not love in word or in tongue, but in deed and in truth. . . . Love one another. . . . Let us love one another, for love is of God. . . . God is love. . . . This is love, not that we loved God, but that He loved us. . . . If we love one another, God abides in us."[11]

This is the "brother" test. Do you love your brothers and sisters in the family of God? Do you enjoy meeting them on weekends for worship? Do you enjoy gathering with them for Bible study? Do you look for ways to tangibly meet their needs? If you just can't haul yourself out of bed on most Sundays to be with your brothers and sisters, that's not a good sign. Those who are truly saved are those who enjoy and bless the household of faith, the family of God.

## The Birthmark of Conflict
### *1 John 5:4*

A fourth sign of being truly saved is conflict. According to 1 John 5:4, "Whatever is born of God overcomes the world. And this is the victory that has overcome the world—our faith." The word *overcome* implies a struggle. We're faced with an adversary whom we must overcome. Our adversary is identified in 1 John 2:14 as the wicked one: "I have written to you, young men, because you are strong, and the word of God abides in you, and you have overcome the wicked one." John went on in the next verses to say: "Do not love the world or the things in the world. . . . For all that *is* in the world—the lust of the flesh, the lust of the eyes, and the pride of life—is not of the Father but is of the world" (1 John 2:15-17).

When you're genuinely born of God, you'll be growing to be an overcomer as you deal with the temptations around you—the world, the flesh, and the devil. You may not be victorious over every temptation every time, but you'll make progress in gaining more victories and losing less battles as you grow stronger in Christ and in the power of the abiding Word of God.

I'll have more about this in the next chapter, but for now I'll tell you that in my own lifelong efforts to be a consistent overcomer, I've found two passages in God's Word to be of particular help. Romans 8:37 says, "In all these things we are more than conquerors through Him who loved us." And 2 Corinthians 2:14 says, "Now thanks *be* to God who always leads us in triumph in Christ." You can claim those as your own in your struggle against temptation.

Have you seen the little anonymous prayer that has been circulating on the Internet? It sums up our struggle in simple terms: "Dear Lord, so far today I am doing all right. I have not gossiped, lost my temper, been greedy, grumpy, nasty, selfish, or self-indulgent. I have not whined, complained, cursed, or eaten any chocolate. I have charged nothing on my credit card. But Lord, I'll be getting out of bed in a minute and I'm going to really need Your help."

Well, we have His help. His commands are promises in reverse, for every command comes with His enabling strength to obey it. We'll not be perfect in this life, but we can live in consistent victory in our conflict with sin. That's our birthright and that's our birthmark.

## The Birthmark of Conduct
### *1 John 5:18*

That leads to the final point I want to make from the first epistle of John. We can see evidence for the validity of salvation in our desire to conduct ourselves in a way that pleases God. According to 1 John 3:9, "Whoever has been born of God does not sin, for His seed remains in him; and he cannot sin, because he has been born of God." The point is repeated in 1 John 5:18: "We know that whoever is born of God does not sin; but he who has been born of God keeps himself, and the wicked one does not touch him."

These verses have puzzled Christians as much as any in the New Testament. If we're not careful, we might interpret them to teach that anyone who is born of God never sins. That would conflict with other passages in the Bible that describe us as fallible and often failing. The only sinlessly perfect person to walk on earth was Jesus Himself. According to James 3:2, "We all stumble in many things."

What, then, did John mean to say in these verses? In using the word *sin* in the passages above, I think he was talking about ongoing rebellion against the law of God. In 1 John 3:4, he said, "Whoever commits sin also commits lawlessness." John was concerned about ongoing conscious and intentional violations of God's law. He was talking about a lifestyle of rebellion. Each day we all sin, omitting things we should do and committing things that we should not do and displaying wrong attitudes. We sin in word, in deed, and in disposition. Does that mean we no longer are saved? No, not at all. But if we are truly saved, we will grieve over our sins, confess them, and seek God's grace to do better.

When we sin and become aware of our sin, we come to the throne of grace in confession, asking God to forgive us as we forsake our sin. John himself made this clear when he wrote, "If we confess our sins, He is faithful and just to forgive us *our* sins and to cleanse us from all unrighteousness. If we say that we have not sinned, we make Him a liar, and His truth is not in us. . . . And if anyone sins, we have an Advocate with the Father, Jesus Christ the righteous" (1 John 1:8 – 2:1).

In 1 John 3:9, the word for sin is a present active infinitive and it describes a continuous action. John is not saying that whoever sins once is not born of God. That would disqualify all of us. It would certainly disqualify me. But John is saying, in effect, "Whoever keeps on willfully sinning, violating God's law with stubborn disregard and ongoing wickedness, cannot have assurance of salvation."

When we are born of God, we have God's seed in us and we inherit His nature, which is in direct conflict with all sin. With His seed and nature within us, we will never become comfortable with sinning. In fact, our lives will increasingly reflect character, integrity, and holiness, for the nature of Jesus Christ will be growing within us. We can learn to overcome temptation and have greater strength and victory as time goes by.

After many years in the ministry and after countless conversations with people who were struggling with

assurance of their salvation, it seems to me that many
people who struggle with assurance fear they have offended
God by committing some sin for which He has not forgiven
them. Despite confession and repentance, they still worry
about whether they are saved. So let me close this chapter
with a story by my friend Max Lucado, who wrote of being
dropped by his insurance company because he had one
too many speeding tickets plus a fender bender. One day
Max received a letter in the mail, informing him to seek
coverage elsewhere. As he reflected on how he wasn't good
enough for his insurance company, the spiritual tie-in
was obvious.

"Many people fear receiving such a letter," Lucado
wrote. "Some worry they already have." Lucado then
imagined a piece of correspondence from the Pearly Gates
Underwriting Division:

> Dear Mrs. Smith,
> I'm writing in response to this morning's request
> for forgiveness. I'm sorry to inform you that you
> have reached your quota of sins. Our records show
> that, since employing our services, you have erred
> seven times in the area of greed, and your prayer
> life is substandard when compared to others of
> like age and circumstance. Further review reveals
> that your understanding of doctrine is in the lower
> 20th percentile and you have excessive tendencies
> to gossip. Because of your sins you are a high-risk
> candidate for heaven. You understand that grace
> has its limits. Jesus sends his regrets and kindest

regards and hopes that you will find some other form of coverage.[12]

We read that with a smile, but it reflects how some people interpret their relationship with the Lord. No, my friend, you don't have to worry about the extent of God's forgiveness or His ability to keep you safely in His hands. Jesus said, "My sheep hear My voice, and I know them, and they follow Me. And I give them eternal life, and they shall never perish; neither shall anyone snatch them out of My hand" (John 10:27-28).

His grace is inexhaustible and His salvation is irreversible. Make sure you have confessed Jesus as your Lord and Savior, and then trust Him with your eternal future. He will never leave you or forsake you. He will never drop you or turn His back to your need. Nothing can separate you from His love, and of that you can be fully persuaded. His Word was given that you might know Jesus Christ as your Savior and that you might know that you have eternal life.

You can know where you're going. You can have assurance of salvation today.

———◇———

# QUESTIONS TO DISCUSS

**1.** Have you ever doubted your salvation? Even now, how would you answer the question, "Do you know for sure if you are going to heaven?" Would you say, "Yes!" or "I hope so!" or "Maybe . . ."? How does God want you to answer that question?

_____

_____

_____

_____

**2.** In 2 Corinthians 13:5, Paul told the Corinthians, "Examine yourselves *as to* whether you are in the faith. Test yourselves." Why did he say this?

_____

_____

_____

_____

**3.** If you've nailed down your confession of Christ as your personal Savior and Lord, how should you respond on those occasions when you don't "feel" saved? What should you tell yourself when doubts arise?

_____

_____

_____

_____

_____

**4.** Of the five birthmarks of true Christians in the book of 1 John—confession, change, compassion, conflict, and conduct—which is strongest in your life? In which area do you need the most work?

_____

_____

_____

_____

_____

**5.** Ongoing disobedience can rob us of a sense of the joy of the assurance of our salvation. What does 1 John 1:9 tell us to do when we become aware of a sin in our lives?

_____

_____

_____

_____

_____

*Blessed assurance, Jesus is mine!*
*O what a foretaste of glory divine!*
*Heir of salvation, purchase of God,*
*Born of His Spirit, washed in His blood.*
*This is my story, this is my song,*
*Praising my Savior, all the day long;*
*This is my story, this is my song,*
*Praising my Savior, all the day long.*

~ Fanny Crosby, in her 1873 hymn "Blessed Assurance"

# CHAPTER TWO

# How Can I Overcome Temptation?

I HEARD ABOUT A YOUNG PRIEST SERVING in the confessional booth for the first time. He was being watched over by an older priest, who was his trainer and mentor. At the end of the first day the older priest took the young man aside and had but one piece of advice for him: "When a person finishes confession, you have got to say something other than 'Wow!'"

When we think of the intensity of sin and the relentless onslaught of temptation, we sometimes want to say, "Wow!" Although human beings have faced temptation since the days of Adam and Eve, sin has never been as accessible as now. Evil has never been as user friendly. Our technologies, mixed with the sinful tendencies of our fallen nature and intensified by Satan, have put a capital $T$ in *Temptation*. Sometimes we wonder whether we can stand against it or whether we'll be swept away like straw huts carried off by a tsunami. It's not just those major red-letter temptations that assault us, for the daily stress of life now has created constant opportunities for us to yield to impatience, irritability, anxiety, profanity, and sharpness of tongue.

I've wondered how the apostle Paul would advise us if he could beam into our time and speak directly to these issues? I believe he would say just what he has already said in God's inspired and timeless Word.

Imagine with me that one day Paul received a letter from a young man who had been recently saved in the ancient city of Corinth. This was an evil city, just as evil as anywhere in today's world. This young man, having found Christ as Savior, had relished God's forgiveness of all his sins. He had rejoiced in becoming a new creation in Christ. But to his astonishment, this fellow had discovered he was still subject to the same temptations that had always dogged him. The evil passions that had controlled his life before conversion were still with him. He was encountering defeat again from the very things for which God had forgiven him. He was still plagued by the same old temptations. He was even beginning to doubt the reality of his conversion and question the true power of God. Now, suppose this young man had written a desperate letter to Paul, asking, "What do I do?"

We don't know of any such letter landing on Paul's desk from a young man as I've described, but we do have Paul's answer to the question I've raised. It is found in a helpful passage in 1 Corinthians 10, and it is one of the Bible's best answers to the question "How can I overcome temptation?"

That's our next question in this book, and it's one of the most frequently repeated questions I'm asked.

The key verse on this subject from Paul's writings is here in 1 Corinthians 10:13, which perhaps you've already memorized. If not, I encourage you to do so now: "No temptation has overtaken you except such as is common to man; but God *is* faithful, who will not allow you to be tempted beyond what you are able, but with the temptation will also make the way of escape, that you may be able to bear *it*."

## The Common Experience of Temptation

First Corinthians 10:13 is comforting because it lets us know of the common experience of temptation. As *The Living Bible* puts it: "Remember this—the wrong desires that come into your life aren't anything new and different. Many others have faced exactly the same problems before you."

Most of us are not surprised to hear of others falling to temptation, but we're often surprised when we face it ourselves. Yet temptation is inevitable. No one escapes it. "You will be tempted," wrote author John White. "The kinds of temptation may change: Candies for kids, sensuality for the young, riches for the middle-aged, and power for the aging. . . . You will be tempted continuously. You will be tempted ferociously at times of crisis. . . . As long as you live you will be tempted."[1]

Perhaps that sounds pessimistic to you, but it's actually reassuring. Whatever you're going through, you're not the only person to pass this way. You're in good company. Countless others have felt the pull of the temptation that now tugs at you. Someone around you is struggling with the same pressures you feel; though, like you, he or she may think they are the only one facing their particular issues. No matter what temptations plague you, they're common to us all.

Even the saints of Scripture struggled mightily with the allurements of sin. Look through your Old Testament and you'll read about Noah's drunkenness, Abraham's deception, Moses' temper, Elijah's murmuring, David's immorality, and Jonah's rebellious spirit. Turning the page to the New Testament you'll see Peter's denial, John Mark's defection, Timothy's anxiety, and Paul's arguing with Barnabas. Every soul who has walked on earth has been tempted. Even Jesus faced temptation. Hebrews 4:15 says, "We do not have a High Priest who cannot sympathize with our weaknesses, but was in all *points* tempted as *we are, yet* without sin."

There once was a little boy standing in front of an apple stand at a grocery store. Spying him, the owner came out and said, "What are you doing, son? Trying to steal one of my apples?"

"No," said the boy, "I'm trying *not* to."

Oh, how we identify with that boy! Temptation is common to all of us, and no temptation has assaulted us but those that are common to everyone.

## The Controlled Environment of Temptation

Even more encouragement comes with the next phrase of 1 Corinthians 10:13: "But God *is* faithful, who will not allow you to be tempted beyond what you are able [to bear]."

The reformer, Martin Luther, had a different way of putting it. He said that we cannot stop birds flying about our heads, but we can prevent them from building a nest in our hair. We'll never be free from temptation until we get to heaven, but our heavenly Father knows how to deliver us from its grasp.

Remember that temptation never comes from God; it's God who provides the way of escape. James 1:13 says, "Let no one say when he is tempted, 'I am tempted by God'; for God cannot be tempted by evil, nor does He Himself tempt anyone." It's the devil who tempts us to evil. He is called "the tempter" in Matthew 4:3 and 1 Thessalonians 3:5.

If you've been a Christian for long, the tempter is no stranger to you. He roars about like a lion, seeking those to devour, and I'm sure he has passed your way more than once. But according to 1 Corinthians 10:13, our faithful God won't allow us to be tempted beyond what we can bear. He may test us, but He never tempts us. When He allows temptation to come into our lives, He promises to limit the kind of test and the intensity of it. He knows our limitations, and He never allows us to be tempted beyond what we can bear. Remember, temptation is not based upon what we think we can handle but upon what God knows we can handle.

The apostle Paul spoke in personal terms about this in 2 Corinthians 1:8-10, when he wrote, "For we do not want you to be ignorant, brethren, of our trouble which came to us in Asia: that we were burdened beyond measure, above strength, so that we despaired even of life. Yes, we had the sentence of death in ourselves that we should not trust in ourselves but in God who raises the dead, who delivered us from so great a death, and does deliver us; in whom we trust that He will still deliver *us.*"

If you read this passage carefully, you will see that Paul uses all three tenses of the word *deliver.* God has delivered us, He is delivering us, and He will yet deliver us. In other words, no matter what situation I'm in, God is there with me. He knows my limitations. He has, can, and will deliver me. Large testing means a large capacity for victory. He knows what each of us is able to endure. There are many uncertainties in the moment of temptation, but there is one uncertainty we can take off the table: God will provide a way of escape.

In 2 Timothy 2:13, Paul adds these reassuring words: "If we are faithless, He remains faithful; He cannot deny Himself." One writer commenting on this verse said, "The faithfulness of God guarantees that no superhuman temptation will enter the life of any believer and that each believer's temptations will be commensurate with his own ability to endure them."[2]

So if you hear someone say, "I was overcome by temptation; it was more than I could stand," don't believe it. That person had better come up with another excuse. God is a faithful Father who will never allow a temptation in my life that is more powerful than His ability to keep me. He maintains a controlled environment for our testing. God will not allow things to go beyond His control and He has not forgotten about us. He controls what enters our lives, knowing the limits of what we can bear.

## The Certain Escape From Temptation

He also gives us a certain escape from temptation. Reviewing 1 Corinthians 10:13 again, we notice God will provide a way of escape, always, every time, in every test, trial, or temptation. The moment the test begins, the way out is available. He doesn't wait to see how we are doing; He provides the means of escape at the outset.

The Greek word Paul used for *escape* has the connotation of a narrow passage out of a treacherous canyon. You might climb down into a canyon and find yourself trapped. But if you look hard enough, you'll find a crevice or a fissure in the wall, perhaps a steep goat path or a small opening that will provide a way to safety.

In a very real sense, Jesus Himself is that way of escape. He said in John 14:6, "I am the way." We may not have sufficient power to resist temptation, but He does. We can't overcome the smallest sin, but He is our victory. He can live His life through us and strengthen us with His indwelling presence. Someone said, "When temptation comes knocking, let Jesus answer the door." That may sound trite, but it conveys a spiritual truth that many people miss. In our own strength we can't overcome temptation, but the Christian life is the Christ-life; it is Christ living His life through us. As we're fully surrendered to Him, filled with

His Spirit, and armed with His Word, His righteousness is manifested through our lives.

In his book *Tempted and Tried*, Russell Moore wrote: "The sheer animal force of temptation ought to remind us of something: the universe is demon haunted. It also ought to remind us there's only one among us who has ever wrestled the demons and prevailed. . . . The same Spirit who led Jesus through the wilderness and empowered him to overcome the Evil One now surges through all of us who are joined by faith to Jesus."[3]

Hebrews 2:18 affirms this, saying, "For in that He Himself has suffered, being tempted, He is able to aid those who are tempted." The escape in the midst of testing is found in the person of Jesus Christ. He's already been down this road. He's experienced temptation, and He wants to secure our total dependence upon Himself.

Nineteenth-century British writer Mark Rutherford gives us these thoughts from his experience: "I am not talking theology or philosophy. I *know* what I am saying, and can point out the times and places when I should have fallen if I had been able to rely for guidance upon nothing better than a commandment or a deduction. But the pure, calm, heroic image of Jesus confronted me, and I succeeded. I had no doubt as to what *He* would have done, and through Him I did not doubt what I ought to do."[4]

Over time I've discovered that temptation isn't so much a matter of what we do but whom we love. Knowing Christ—really knowing Him, not simply knowing *about* Him—changes everything. More often than not, we tap into divine power in the time of temptation because we've filled our minds with Him and there is no room for the world's cheap substitutes.

But let me say something else about "the way of escape." While this is a very encouraging promise, it must not be taken for granted. In most situations the way of escape will be just a fleeting thought: *This is wrong! Don't do it!* The way of escape may only last a moment, and if not taken, it will be too late.

There's a great illustration of this in the writing of Presbyterian pastor Bryan Chapell, who said, "The air war over Bosnia in the late 1990s made famous the escape of Scott O'Grady. The downed American flier evaded capture for days in enemy territory until rescue helicopters found him. When the helicopter landed in the clearing near where O'Grady was hiding, he didn't relax in the brush and say, 'I wish that the pilot would have landed a little closer.' He shook off the fatigue, fought through the bushes, drew his weapon and, with every ounce of energy he had, ran to the escape that had been provided for him. His actions parallel the engagement God requires of us in spiritual warfare. We should not assume that, because God promises to provide a way out of temptation, we have no role in our own rescue. God always provides a way of escape, but he may also require great effort from us."[5]

Ethel Edison, who lives in a Florida retirement village, recalls learning to apply Scriptural truth at the age of fifteen. "When I was a teenager," she said, "my mother and I lived alone; she was divorced and we were very worldly people. I was already five-foot-eight and could pass for twenty-one. Mother and I would go on double dates with servicemen.

The kids in high school rejected me because I didn't date peers; I went with soldiers. Then through the ministry of a local church I became a Christian. A nearby lady who worked with Child Evangelism Fellowship told me I must learn 1 Corinthians 10:13. She emphasized the word *must*, knowing of my environment and lifestyle. I looked it up and thought it contained too many words and phrases to memorize. But I worked until I learned it: 'No temptation has overtaken you except such as is common to man; but God is faithful, who will not allow you to be tempted beyond what you are able, but with the temptation will also make the way of escape, that you may be able to bear it.'

"The power of that verse kept me from the temptations I faced as a new Christian. My biggest worry was my boyfriend, a soldier in the army, and I didn't know what to say to him. But that same week he was transferred and taken out of my life. The Lord was applying 1 Corinthians 10:13 to my experience, even as I was working to do my part in applying it."

Ethel continued, "Three months later my mother was converted. Shortly afterward was New Year's Eve, which had always been the biggest night in the year for us. This year we skipped the parties and went to church. When Mother got home she realized she had not once thought about what she would have been doing in the world, and after that she had no doubt she was truly a Christian. God had given us both a way of escape."

Ethel later became a career missionary in Africa.[6]

## Biblical Principles to Help You Overcome Temptation

In view of 1 Corinthians 10:13, let me give you some biblical techniques for overcoming temptation.

First, we must recognize the possibility of temptation. Expect it. The verse just before 1 Corinthians 10:13 says, "Therefore let him who thinks he stands take heed lest he fall" (verse 12). We shouldn't let our guard down or somehow expect to be immune from the assault of Satan. Sometimes the worst temptations hit us right after a victory or a high moment in our lives. We can't assume we're beyond temptation's reach. We're vulnerable every minute so we have to remain diligent all the time. Elijah faced his worst defeat right after his greatest victory, which occurred when he called fire down from heaven on Mount Carmel (1 Kings 18 – 19). Peter made one of his worst mistakes immediately after one of his greatest moments (Matthew 16:15-23). King David was at the height of his career when he fell into moral sin (2 Samuel 11).

Jesus said, "Watch and pray, lest you enter into temptation. The spirit indeed *is* willing, but the flesh *is* weak" (Matthew 26:41). Pride is Satan's number one strategy, and it will get you into trouble every time. Proverbs 16:18 says, "Pride *goes* before destruction, and a haughty spirit before a fall." Don't start thinking you're something special. Be careful about listening to good comments from others. Thank God for any positive reinforcement you receive, but don't dwell in it. Keep moving forward. As soon as you climb to the top of the mountain you're in danger of falling off. Be careful; watch out for occasions when Satan can get to you.

That brings up my second suggestion. Request help in advance of temptation. Jesus taught us to pray in the Lord's Prayer, "Lead us not into temptation, but deliver us from the evil one" (Matthew 6:13, NIV). In our devotional times we need to ask God to prepare us for victory over the temptation that will surely come our way. This is a spiritual discipline we can develop in our lives to get us through a time of testing.

I'm going to put this in very practical terms. When I served as a youth pastor years ago, I told my young people, "Don't wait until you're in the backseat of a steamy car to decide your views about premarital sex. You'd better establish your convictions and principles before you get into a situation where compromise is possible. Decide in advance what you believe about the important things in life, and ask God to give you victory over temptation before it comes."

The great Bible teacher of yesteryear, Dr. R. A. Torrey, said, "The reason why many fail in the battle is because they wait until the hour of battle. The reason why others succeed is because they have gained their victory on their knees long before the battle came. . . . Anticipate your battles, fight them on your knees before temptation comes, and you will always have victory."[7]

My third technique for overcoming temptation comes directly from James 4:7-8: "Resist the devil and he will flee from you. Draw near to God and He will draw near to you." This is a two-fold command. As we draw near to God and resist the devil, we can have victory over temptation. Jesus resisted the devil by quoting memorized Scripture, and that's our strongest offensive weapon—the double-edged sword of the Spirit. Find a set of Bible verses that speak to your points of vulnerability. Memorize them, meditate on them, and keep them unsheathed for ready use.

We also have to learn to retreat from certain things that Satan throws out like bait, trying to lure us into sin. There is a time to resist and a time to retreat. Mark Twain once said: "There are several good protections against temptations, but the surest is cowardice."[8] I'm not sure "cowardice" is the best word,

> *"Whatever your heart clings to and confides in, that is really your God."*[9]
>
> ~ MARTIN LUTHER

but the sentiment is correct. The Word of God tells us to run away from certain kinds of temptation rather than stand toe to toe to fight them.

For example, the Bible tells us, "Therefore, my beloved, flee from idolatry" (1 Corinthians 10:14). An idol is anything that comes between you and God. Anything of value to you could be an idol. When you begin to realize that something is taking the place of God in your life, you don't need to sit and ponder it. You don't need to write a thesis or call a meeting about it. You need to flee, to turn to Christ as absolute Lord over every affection in your life.

The Bible also commands, "Flee sexual immorality. Every sin that a man does is outside the body, but he who commits sexual immorality sins against his own body" (1 Corinthians 6:18). In 2 Timothy 2:22, we're told: "Flee also youthful lusts; but pursue righteousness, faith, love, peace." Peter also tells us to "abstain from fleshly lusts which war against the soul" (1 Peter 2:11).

Sexual temptation is a demonic trump card; there's something unique and terrible about its power. The devil uses it for those in ministry, marriage, and those maturing. But the Old Testament example of Joseph, when he fled from the sexual advances of his master's wife, teaches us the value of running away from sin and temptation.

A young staff member in a church was finding it difficult to deal with the flirtations of a woman in the congregation. On one occasion he found himself in the awkward position of having to be present in a ladies meeting where this woman would be seated next to him. Since he did not know what to do, he went to his senior pastor and asked for advice. He said, "Pastor, there will be many people at this event. Don't you think there is safety in numbers?"

"Well, yes," said the pastor, "there is some safety in Numbers but there is more safety in Exodus."

When it comes to dangerous temptation, take the exit ramp. Flee. Abstain. As much as possible, reduce your exposure to danger zones.

The Bible also commands us to flee from greed. Paul wrote, "The love of money is a root of all *kinds of* evil, for which some have strayed from the faith in their greediness, and pierced themselves through with many sorrows. But you, O man of God, flee these things" (1 Timothy 6:10-11). All kinds of evils proceed from the mouth of materialism. Don't let greed get its hooks into your life or the lives of your children. And when you flee temptation, don't leave a forwarding address.

That leads to my fifth suggestion for overcoming temptation. Remove any means of sin far from you. The writer of Proverbs was constantly giving this kind of advice to his son and to his readers. For example, Proverbs 4:14-15 says, "Do not enter the path of the wicked, and do not walk in the way of evil. Avoid it, do not travel on it; turn away from it and pass on." The apostle Paul put this in New Testament terms when he told the Romans, "But put on the Lord Jesus Christ, and make no provision for the flesh, to *fulfill its* lust" (Romans 13:14).

Instead of setting ourselves up for failure, we should get rid of the things in our lives that cause us to be defeated. When you remove sin far from you, you'll be amazed at how much more victorious you will be. Learn to replace bad influences with good ones. Proverbs 13:20 says, "He who walks with wise *men* will be wise, but the companion of fools will be destroyed." If you have friends who drag you down into sin every time you see them, perhaps you need a new set of friends. Ask yourself: Are the people I'm hanging out with moving me toward God or are they pulling me away from Him?

Resolve to live on the high road. Every Christian has a choice to make. The high road is the uncompromising walk with God that doesn't count any cost too high if it will lead to God's ultimate blessing on our lives. The low road is the path of convenience and compromise. If we've slipped into tolerance of sin, we've gradually gotten on the low road. If we're continually yielding to temptation, we're on the low road. But the Word of God gives us the information we need to get back onto the high road where the Lord wants us. If we obey His Word, we can experience victory over temptation. We can live on a higher plane.

Dr. David Martyn Lloyd-Jones wrote: "There are certain things in this life that are patently opposed to God and His righteousness. There is no question about that at all. We know they are bad; we know they are harmful; we know they are sinful. . . To hunger and thirst after righteousness means avoiding such things just as we would avoid the very plague itself. . . But it does not stop at that . . . If we are truly hungering and thirsting after righteousness, we shall avoid even those things that tend to dull or take the edge off our spiritual appetite. There are so many things that are quite harmless in themselves, and which are perfectly legitimate, yet if you find you are spending much of your time with them, and that you desire the things of God less, you must avoid them. I think it is a common sense argument." [10]

My final suggestion on overcoming temptation is to refocus your thoughts and affections. The way for us to deal with temptation is not to grit our teeth and make up our minds that we will not do a certain thing. The key is to fill our minds with other things. Instead of simply resisting, refocus your thoughts. Remember:

- *Every temptation comes to us via our thoughts.* [11]
  —ERWIN LUTZER

- *The mind of man is the battleground on which every moral and spiritual battle is fought.* [12]
  —J. OSWALD SANDERS

- *Our defeat or victory begins with what we think,*
  *and if we guard our thoughts we shall not have*
  *much trouble anywhere else along the line.*[13]
—Vance Havner

In his book *The Obedience Option*, David Hegg tells of a time he was talking to a young man who claimed he couldn't stop his pattern of sleeping with different women. The young man knew it was wrong, but he also claimed that his sexual lust was inevitable. That justified it in his mind. He even pointed out that God had created him with very strong desires and urges.

After listening to this explanation, Hegg interrupted the fellow and said, "Suppose that I came into your room and caught you and your girlfriend as you were just starting this 'inevitable' process. Suppose I took out ten one-hundred-dollar bills, and told you that they were yours if you [stopped]. What would you do?"

When the young man quickly said he'd rather have the cash, Hegg asked, "So what happened to the irresistible force of lust?"

> *When you flee temptation, be sure you don't leave a forwarding address.*

Then Hegg concluded, "We both realized a very simple truth: one passion may seem irresistible until a greater passion comes along. . . . If we take this principle into the arena of righteous living, it comes out like this: The only way to overcome a passion for sin is with an overwhelming passion for righteousness.

This overwhelming passion for righteousness is actually a mindset that the Bible calls faith. Here is a helpful definition of this kind of overwhelming faith: Faith is a life-dominating conviction that all God has for me through obedience is better by far than anything Satan can offer me through selfishness and sin."[14]

Anyone who has trained a dog to obey knows how this works. A bit of meat or bread is placed on the floor near the dog and the master says, "No!" The dog knows he must not touch it. The dog will usually take his eyes off the food, because the temptation to disobey is too great. He will instead fix his eyes on the master's face.

The Bible frequently draws lessons for us from the animal world, and here is a lesson we can learn from the dog. Always look to the Master's face. The Bible says, "If then you were raised with Christ, seek those things which are above, where Christ is, sitting at the right hand of God. Set your mind on things above, not on things on the earth" (Colossians 3:1-2).

When I speak at men's retreats about these things, I tell them to keep the face of their heavenly Master in front of them, along with the face of their bride, their children, and their grandchildren. Ask yourself, "Really, is it worth ruining everything in my life for a moment of pleasure when, in doing it, I will deny the Master whom I love and my friends and my family who look to me for an example?"

We don't have to be victimized by temptation. Our Almighty God has given us a Book filled with ammunition to ward off the attacks of the world, the flesh, and the devil.

Let's be doers of the Word and not hearers only. The Bible was given to us for holiness and righteousness.

Learn to hide God's Word in your heart that you may not sin against Him.

———○———

# QUESTIONS TO DISCUSS

**1.** Think of the fictional young Corinthian man who might have written to the apostle Paul, confused that he was still struggling with temptations after his conversion. Have you ever felt that way? If that young man had asked you for advice, what would you have told him?

_____

_____

_____

_____

_____

**2.** Why is it sometimes so hard for us to find that "way of escape" promised in 1 Corinthians 10:13?

_____

_____

_____

_____

**3.** In addition to 1 Corinthians 10:13, what are some other Bible verses that have been of greatest help to you in fighting the temptations you face?

_____

_____

_____

**4.** What's the difference between temptation and sin? Can we have one without the other?

_____

_____

_____

_____

_____

**5.** Describe a time when God truly gave you victory over some temptation you were facing. What truths or techniques enabled you to claim that victory?

_____

_____

_____

_____

_____

*"Beware of your best moments as well as of your worst, or rather the moments which succeed the best: they are the most perilous of all. Just when the consciousness of a triumph seems to permit and justify disarmament for a moment, the subtle foe with whom you have to deal will steal in on you and win a treacherous victory."*[15]

~ J. B. Brown

# CHAPTER THREE

# How Can I Get Victory Over Worry?

A NERVOUS AIRLINE PASSENGER BEGAN PACING the terminal when bad weather delayed his departure. During his walk, he came across a life insurance machine that offered $100,000 in the event of an untimely death aboard his flight. The policy was just three dollars. He looked through the window at the threatening clouds and thought of his family at home. For that price it seemed foolish not to buy the policy, so he took out the coverage. He then looked for a place to eat and settled on a Chinese restaurant. It was a relaxing meal until he opened his fortune cookie, which read, "Your recent investment will pay big dividends."

We may smile at the disconcerted traveler, but we all battle those nagging concerns that disturb our sense of inner peace. Our lives are full of concern, and sometimes these concerns have a way of morphing into monsters of the mind. Worry is *concern* on steroids. It attacks our peace of heart, assaults our faith, ties our intestines in knots, fills our minds with shadows, and sends flaming darts to pierce our emotional wellbeing.

In a December 2013 article entitled "Surviving Anxiety," author and journalist Scott Stossel described his own battle with worry in a way that strikes a common chord: "Anxiety has afflicted me all my life. When I was a child and my mother was attending law school at night, I spent evenings at home with a babysitter, abjectly terrified that my parents had died in a car crash or had abandoned me . . . During first grade, I spent nearly every afternoon for months in the school nurse's office . . . begging to go home . . . During high school, I would purposely lose tennis [matches] to escape the agony of anxiety that competitive situations would provoke in me.

"In short, I have, since the age of about 2, been a twitchy bundle of phobias, fears, and neuroses . . . Here's what I've tried: individual psychotherapy (three decades of it), family therapy, group therapy, cognitive-behavioral therapy, rational emotive behavior therapy, acceptance and commitment therapy, hypnosis, meditation . . . self-help workbooks, massage therapy, prayer, acupuncture, yoga, Stoic philosophy, and audiotapes I ordered off a late-night TV infomercial. And medication. Lots of medication. Thorazine. Imipramine. Desipramine. Nardil . . . BuSpar. Prozac. Zoloft. Paxil. Wellbutrin. Effexor. Celexa. Lexapro. Cymbalta. Luvox. Trazodone. Levoxyl. Inderal. Tranxene. Serax. Centrax. St. John's Wort. Zolpidem. Valium. Librium. Ativan. Xanax. Klonopin. Also: beer, wine, gin, bourbon, vodka, and scotch. Here's what's worked: Nothing."[1]

## Defining Worry

Well, if I could sit down and chat with that poor worrier, I would like to direct him to the passage of Scripture I'm recommending to you. It's a passage that has helped me whenever I've been in the grip of anxiety. It's a portion of Scripture from the Sermon on the Mount, and it serves as the definitive prescription of Jesus Christ, the Great Physician, for our worry, anxiety, and for our daily walk of faith. In this passage—Matthew 6:25-34—Jesus said, "Therefore I say to you, do not worry . . . So why do you worry . . .? Do not worry. . . . Do not worry. . . ."

Let's begin by looking at the word Jesus used for *worry*. What exactly is this troubling attitude? Everyone has their own way of describing it. The dictionary defines *worry* as "a set of thoughts that causes us to feel troubled or uneasy, distressed, anxious, or apprehensive."

A host of sages have provided more vivid definitions. Most of these are proverbs that have been around and are variously attributed to different people; but all of them reveal a different aspect of our anxious thoughts.

- *Worry is an old man with bended head, carrying a load of feathers which he thinks are lead.*

- *Worrying is like a rocking chair. It gives you something to do but doesn't get you anywhere.*

- *Worry is the misuse of your God-given imagination.*

- *Worry is putting question marks where God has put periods.*

- *Worry is the interest we pay on tomorrow's troubles.*

- *Worry is a form of atheism because it assumes there's no God watching over us.*

- *Worry is faith in the negative.*

- *Worry is an emotional spasm which occurs when the mind catches hold of something and will not let it go.*

Much of our worry concerns the future. When we worry, we're often fretting about something we can do nothing about. The future is not here and the future is not ours. We can't control the future nor predict what it will look like. Only God knows the future, so when we worry we're letting our minds get torn apart over something we cannot control.

How does the Bible define worry? The Greek word that is translated *worry* in Matthew 6 is *merimnao*, and it comes from two smaller terms: *merizo*, which means "to divide"; and *nous* which means "mind." The idea is "being drawn or pulled in different directions, being torn apart." So worrying is like having your spirit pulled apart, having a mind divided between legitimate thoughts and destructive ones. It reminds us of James 1:8, which calls the doubter "a double-minded man, unstable in all his ways."

Jesus warned Martha against such double-mindedness. Her story is recorded in Luke 10:41-42, which says that as she flew around the house working and fretting and fussing, Jesus said to her, "Martha, Martha, you are worried and troubled about many things. But one thing is needed, and Mary has chosen that good part, which will not be taken away from her."

Lots of us are Marthas. We fly around, worried and troubled about many things. We also live in a world that makes it easy to worry. When we read the news and watch troubling reports from around the globe, we realize we have a lot of valid reasons to worry about the future. But as biblical Christians we have better reasons *not* to worry. So when we succumb to worry, it is both emotionally distressing and spiritually detrimental.

In His Parable of the Sower in Matthew 13, the Lord described a sower who went out to broadcast seeds. Some of the seeds fell among thorns. Jesus added, "The thorns sprang up and choked them" (verse 7). Later, down in verse 22 of the same chapter, He interpreted His figure of speech: "Now he who received seed among the thorns is he who hears the word, and the cares of this world and the deceitfulness of riches choke the word, and he becomes unfruitful."

Worry can choke the Word of God in our lives and render us unfruitful. It can tear our thoughts apart and make us double-minded doubters. That's why in Matthew 6:25-34, Jesus said, "Therefore I say to you, do not worry. . . . So why do you worry . . .? Do not worry. . . . Do not worry."

When Jesus said, "Do not worry," He was not telling us to forgo planning. Jesus Himself spent forty days in the wilderness thinking through the ministry He would perform (Matthew 4:1-11). He planned ahead for a Last Supper (Luke 22:7-13), and He planned for the disciples to continue His mission after He was gone (Matthew 28:16-20). Nor was He telling us to live without concern. If we saw one of our children playing in the street, we'd have every reason to be concerned. Concern is a legitimate emotion that allows us to focus on a problem and resolve it. Concern usually involves a clear-headed response to a present need. Worry is an unhealthy response to a future fear. You don't need to worry about being concerned, but you should be concerned about worrying.

## Understanding Worry

When we define worry as we've done, we can better understand it. In Matthew 6:25-32, Jesus shared several things He wanted His listeners to realize. He taught them, for example, that worry is inconsistent. Verse 25 says, "Therefore I say to you, do not worry about your life, what you will eat or what you will drink; nor about your body, what you will put on. Is not life more than food and the body more than clothing?"

This is an argument from the greater to the lesser. Our Lord was saying, in effect: "Listen carefully, you who worry about the necessities of life like food and clothing. The One on whom you are depending is the One who has given you life. If He has created your very life, don't you think He can care for the simple things that adorn your life? If our God has the power to create these marvelous organisms we call our bodies, isn't it logical to believe He can provide clothes to put on our bodies, food to put in them, and shelter to put over them? Cannot the One who has done the greater also do the lesser?"

If you believe God is your Creator, you should also believe He is your Sustainer. Otherwise you're inconsistent in your beliefs.

In verse 26, Jesus went on to say, "Look at the birds of the air, for they neither sow nor reap nor gather into barns; yet your heavenly Father feeds them. Are you not of more value than they?" In my mind's eye, I can see Him pausing at this point during the Sermon on the Mount and pointing to a flock of birds flying overhead.

Here the argument goes from the lesser to the greater. If God can take care of lesser things like birds, can He not take care of great things—like you and me? God designed every sparrow, robin, blackbird, chickadee, eagle, parrot, and hummingbird. He delights in His creative genius, and He's aware of every single stroke of the wing. Not one of His creatures falls to the ground without His notice. But as wonderful, colorful, and songful as they are, the birds of the air are not as valuable as you.

I love these two verses, Matthew 6:25-26, because they teach both sides of the same truth. If God can do the greater (give us life), He can do the lesser (provide for our needs). And if He gladly does the lesser (caring for the birds), will He not do the greater (caring for me)?

Our Lord's reasoning is logical and flawless. He was so eager for us to grasp this line of thinking that He repeated

His point on another occasion, in Matthew 10:29-31: "Are not two sparrows sold for a copper coin? And not one of them falls to the ground apart from your Father's will. . . . Do not fear therefore; you are of more value than many sparrows."

A copper coin was the Jewish measurement known as the *assarion*, which was worth one-sixteenth of a *denarius*. Since a denarius represented a day's wages in the time of Jesus, a copper coin was one-sixteenth of a day's wages. You could get a couple of sparrows for a copper coin. They were inexpensive. Yet they are extremely valuable to God and not one of them is overlooked by His divine care. Since we are of infinitely greater value than sparrows, shouldn't we have confidence in God's willingness to look after us and care for our interests?

There's a little poem, evidently written for children in the 1800s, that sometimes appears under the title "Overheard in an Orchard." It brings our Lord's point right down to where we're living.

> Said the Robin to the Sparrow,
> "I should really like to know
> Why these anxious human beings
> Rush about and worry so."
>
> Said the Sparrow to the Robin,
> "Friend, I think that it must be
> That they have no Heavenly Father
> Such as cares for you and me."[2]

One of the interesting observations about this passage on worry in Matthew 6 is that it's found in the middle of a discussion about material things. It's evident from observing life that material possessions add to the worry chart for most people who have them. Whenever we place too much faith in material things and not enough faith in Christ, we will begin to worry about survival and about many other things. This is why Jesus said earlier in the passage, "No one can serve two masters; for either he will hate the one and love the other, or else he will be loyal to the one and despise the other. You cannot serve God and mammon" (Matthew 6:24).

As we continue reading our passage in Matthew 6, we come to our Lord's next point in verse 27. Worry, He indicates, is ineffective. "Which of you by worrying can add one cubit to his stature?" There are two ways to interpret this. The basic idea conveyed in the original text is: "Which of you by worrying can add length to himself?" Translators and commentators are divided as to whether Jesus was talking about length of stature or length of days.

If He was talking about physical height, then His argument was, "Can worry add a cubit (approximately eighteen inches) to your height? Can you grow an extra foot-and-a-half by worrying about your stature? Of course not. And it's just as futile to worry about the future as it is to stand around all day worrying that you're not taller than you are."

Many New Testament scholars, however, believe Jesus was referring to length of days. In this case, the argument would sound like this: "Which of you by worrying can add one day or minute to your life span?" The answer is no one. Worrying cannot help us live longer, but it may very well shorten our lives. We can certainly subtract days from our lifespan by worrying. One man observed, "There are undoubtedly graves all over America where lie the sleeping bodies of truly believing people who cheated God out of ten, and perhaps fifteen or more, years of life because they worried themselves into their graves ahead of time. Which of you by being anxious can add? Nobody! Which of you by being anxious can subtract? Everybody!"[3]

We cannot worry ourselves into a taller stature or into a longer life. Worrying, therefore, is illogical and ineffective.

Jesus went on to say, "So why do you worry about clothing? Consider the lilies of the field, how they grow: they neither toil nor spin; and yet I say to you that even Solomon in all his glory was not arrayed like one of these. Now if God so clothes the grass of the field, which today is, and tomorrow is thrown into the oven, will He not much more clothe you, O you of little faith?" (Matthew 6:28-30)

Here again I think Jesus may have paused in His sermon to point to some wildflowers in the meadow where He was preaching. Perhaps He stooped over and plucked a simple bloom. There in His hands was a gem of color, a blossom worthy of being painted by the greatest artist on earth. It's a preacher. It can teach us a lesson about trusting God for clothing. The flowers do not toil nor do they spin; yet the heavenly Father clothes them. King Solomon in all his glory never had such rich apparel as a simple wildflower.

If the flowers of the field, which quickly wither and fade and have no eternal quality, are adequately cared for, what about us? We should never doubt that the Father in heaven will care for our needs in this world. If God takes such good care of the beauty of the flowers of the field, which have a very short lifespan, doesn't it make sense that He will take care of you who are eternal?

The bottom line? From God's eternal perspective, worry is inconsistent, irrational, ineffective, illogical, and irresponsible. Matthew 6:31-32 sums it up, saying, "Therefore do not worry, saying, 'What shall we eat?' or 'What shall we drink?' or 'What shall we wear?' For after all these things the Gentiles seek. For your heavenly Father knows that you need all these things."

When you're tempted to worry, then, you should stop long enough to ask, "Who am I anyway? Am I a child of God or am I an unbeliever?"

In verses 31 and 32, when Jesus said that the "Gentiles" were worried about what they would eat or drink or wear, He referred to people who did not have a relationship with the Father. They were unbelievers. Some translations use the word *pagans*. So when we succumb to worry, we act like those who bow down to gods of wood and stone.

> *"To think the Lord who clothes lilies will leave his own children naked is shameful. O little faith, learn better manners!"*[4]
> ~ CHARLES H. SPURGEON

Pagans choose gods for themselves that don't see, think, feel, care, or watch over those who worship them. Their gods can't really help them. Their gods can't provide for their needs. When you, as a child of the true God, yield to anxiety, you act like a pagan. That's a form of unbelief, for you have a Father in heaven who loves you and knows your needs before you even ask Him for your daily bread.

That's the way Jesus viewed worry in this passage, and that's how He wants us to understand it.

## Overcoming Worry

After defining worry and helping us to understand its nature, Jesus ends His emphasis in Matthew 6 by telling us how to overcome it. He has a two-fold plan. This is the simplest and most affective antidote to worry ever prescribed.

First, Jesus said, you must totally commit your life to Him. In our discussion of this chapter, we're now coming to one of the great verses of the Bible—verse 33: "But seek first the kingdom of God and His righteousness, and all these things shall be added to you." Instead of worrying about food, drink, and dress, Jesus commands us to seek first the kingdom of God and His righteousness.

I urge you to offer yourself as a living sacrifice to God. Put Christ first. Trust Him with your life, with all your needs, with the concerns of yesterday, today, and tomorrow. With all your heart, live for Him who is the same yesterday, today, and forever. That's the first change you need to make if you hope to overcome worry.

Missionary Hudson Taylor said, "Let us give up our work, our thoughts, our plans, ourselves, our lives, our loved ones, our influence, our all, right into His hand, and then, when we have given all over to Him, there will be nothing left for us to be troubled about, or to make trouble about."[5]

As we seek first His kingdom and His righteousness, He promises to provide for all our needs, saying, "all these things shall be added to you." Richard Greene of Cary, North Carolina, learned this lesson while in college. He was fretting over bills one day, trying to balance his checkbook. He grew agitated and afraid. "Where will the extra money come from?" he asked aloud. "Please, Lord, help me pay these bills."

As he finished balancing his checkbook, he noticed the final digits on his pocket calculator—6.33. He had six dollars, thirty-three cents left. Suddenly he remembered Matthew 6:33. He laughed and took it as a message from the Lord. Shortly afterward, he received an unexpected scholarship. A little later a friend handed him a check for his month's rent. God provided his needs throughout college, and later Richard became director of public relations for Trans World Radio, beaming the message of Scripture (including Matthew 6:33) around the world.[6]

This is the first part of our Lord's plan, committing our work, our thoughts, our plans, ourselves—everything—totally to Jesus Christ. But there is a second step, which is found in the next verse, Matthew 6:34. Having committed our lives to Him, we must concentrate our energies on living one day at a time: "Therefore do not worry about tomorrow, for tomorrow will worry about its own things. Sufficient for the day is its own trouble."

If verse 33 gives us the long view (committing the whole of life to the Lord), verse 34 gives us the short view (living one day at a time for the Lord). The British pastor John Stott said it this way, "One day's trouble is enough for one day or each day has troubles enough of its own. So why anticipate them? If we do, we double them. For if our fear does not materialize, we have worried once for nothing; if it does materialize, we have worried twice instead of once. In both cases it is foolish: worry doubles trouble."[7]

The trouble with worrying so much about your security in the future is that it makes you feel so insecure in the present. Jesus told us not to dwell on our tomorrows. He was echoing the truth of Deuteronomy 33:25, which says, "As your days, so shall your strength be." Each day has its own needs and its own supplies. Every day has a burden that belongs to that particular day. Don't borrow tomorrow's burden before tomorrow, and don't try to do tomorrow's work today. Worry doesn't empty tomorrow of its sorrow, but it does empty today of its strength.

In preaching on this subject, I've occasionally used a tender story from World War II. At the close of that terrible conflict, the Allies gathered up hungry, homeless war orphans and put them into camps, providing sufficient clothing and food. Understandably, some of the youngsters had trouble sleeping at night. They were fitful and afraid. They were conditioned by hunger, and that left them restless.

One of the doctors hit upon the idea of placing a slice of fresh bread into the hand of each child as he or she got into bed. This was not to be eaten but to be held for the next morning. This habit seemed to relax the children and they began sleeping much better. The reason is apparent.

The children, having known terrible hunger, had been concerned about where the next meal was coming from. Now they could go to sleep without worrying about tomorrow's needs. The crust of bread in their hands was the assurance of their next meal.

You can be sure your heavenly Father has made provision for your tomorrow, for He has filled your life with tokens of His goodness and faithfulness today. Lamentations 3:23 reminds us that God's compassions are new every morning. Every bird in the sky and every flower of the field is a testimony from heaven to us, saying, "Trust Me. I will care for you day by day. Seek Me first, and all these things will be added to you."[8]

Don't worry about yesterday's sins; God has forgiven them. Don't worry about yesterday's successes; God has recorded them. Don't worry about yesterday's sorrows; God can heal them and point us forward. We're to live life on a daily basis.

Years ago motivational expert Dale Carnegie wrote a famous self-help book entitled *How to Stop Worrying and Start Living*. He didn't write this book from an evangelical perspective, but his very first chapter was based on the words of Jesus in Matthew 6, on the subject of not worrying about tomorrow. Carnegie summarized this principle in a simple little rule: "Live in 'Day-Tight Compartments.'"

He said, "You and I are standing this very second at the meeting place of two eternities: the vast past . . . and the future . . . We can't possibly live in either of those eternities—no, not even for one split second. But, by trying to do so, we can wreck both our bodies and our minds. So let's be content to live the only time we can possibly live: from now until bedtime. . . . Live in day-tight compartments."[9]

Warren Wiersbe said, "Most Christians are being crucified on a cross between two thieves: yesterday's regrets and tomorrow's worries."[10] It's God's will that we focus our attention on the present, remembering that He promised to be with us at all times. Recall the Lord's words at the burning bush in Exodus 3:14. When Moses asked God about His name, the Lord replied, "I AM WHO I AM." God is the self-existent Creator who dwells in eternity, yet He is always present with us in the *now*. He is I AM, always "present tense" in our lives.

A pastor was on a long haul flight when the voice of the captain came across the speakers. "Ladies and gentlemen, please fasten your seat belts. I'm asking the flight attendants to be seated and we're suspending beverage service because we're expecting turbulence ahead."

Turbulence is what they got. Within minutes, the plane was trembling, then quaking from the storm. Cracks of thunder could be heard above the roar of the engines. Lightning lit up the darkening skies, and the plane was like a cork tossed around on a heavenly ocean. One moment the airplane was lifted on terrific currents of air; the next, it dropped as if about to crash. The pastor was as terrified as the other passengers. Only one person seemed perfectly calm, a little girl, her feet tucked beneath her as she curled up reading a book amid the mayhem. Sometimes she closed her eyes as if napping.

Gradually the plane escaped the storm and finally flew peacefully on to its destination. While waiting to disembark, the pastor couldn't help asking the girl why she had not worried. "My daddy's the pilot," she said, "and he's taking me home. I didn't worry because I knew he was in the cockpit."[11]

In the midst of the storm, we need to look up and notice that the cockpit is occupied. Almighty God is at the controls. We can rest secure in Him as He takes us home. Though our world is suffering turbulence and though severe turbulence occurs in our lives, we know the Pilot. Isaiah 26:3 is a prayer for us to echo: "You will keep *him* in perfect peace, *whose* mind *is* stayed *on You*, because he trusts in You."

The past is under the blood of Christ, and the future is in the hands of God, and He is your I AM, with you right now as you seek first His kingdom and live for Him day by day. This is the day the Lord has made and we can rejoice and be glad in it. "Therefore I say to you, do not worry . . . So why do you worry . . .? Do not worry. . . . Do not worry."

Peace is God's supernatural gift for our hearts. If a trickle of fear is meandering through your mind and cutting a deep channel, unleash the flood of God's peace. He is in control. He is in His holy temple and on His mighty throne. He will pilot your life. He can bear the load and grant you peace as you totally commit yourself to Him and concentrate your energies on living one day at a time for Christ and His glory.

———o———

# QUESTIONS TO DISCUSS

**1.** Take a moment to compose your own personal definition of worry. How would you describe it from your own experience?

_____

_____

_____

_____

_____

**2.** Jesus told us to look at the sparrows and lilies. What other items could we study to reassure ourselves of God's care for us?

_____

_____

_____

_____

_____

**3.** This chapter has focused on what Jesus said about worry in Matthew 6:25-34, but several other passages of the Bible deal with the subjects of fear, worry, and anxiety. What are some of your favorite verses on this subject? Hint: You might check out Psalm 37 and Philippians 4.

_____

_____

_____

_____

**4.** Do you find it hard to live in "day-tight compartments"? How would you advise a friend to begin learning this biblical habit?

_____

_____

_____

_____

_____

**5.** What most worries you about the future? Can you think of a verse of Scripture that speaks to that specific concern?

_____

_____

_____

_____

*"So my counsel is: Don't worry about things—food, drink, and clothes. For you already have life and a body—and they are far more important than what to eat and wear. Look at the birds! They don't worry about what to eat—they don't need to sow or reap or store up food—for your heavenly Father feeds them. And you are far more valuable to him than they are. Will all your worries add a single moment to your life? And why worry about your clothes? Look at the field lilies! They don't worry. . . . So don't worry. . . . So don't be anxious about tomorrow. God will take care of your tomorrow too. Live one day at a time."*

~ Jesus, in Matthew 6:25-34 (*The Living Bible*)

# CHAPTER FOUR

# How Can I Find Forgiveness?

IN ONE OF HIS IMITABLE STORIES, Pastor Max Lucado wrote about a man named Stewart who caused a terrible accident that took the life of an eighteen-year-old woman named Susan. Despite the tragedy, Stewart felt he had gotten off easy, at least at first, at least legally. He'd been driving drunk and had plowed into Susan's car on a New Year's morning in New York. She had died instantly. Stewart was convicted of manslaughter and drunken driving; but on top of his criminal trial, Susan's family had won a civil suit against him. They requested an unusual and creative judgment. At first they had sued Stewart for $1.5 million, but in the end they decided they only wanted $936.

The money was to be paid in a specific way. Each Friday, the day Susan died, Stewart was to make out a check in her name for one dollar and mail it to the family. The amount was to be paid one dollar per week for eighteen years, one for each year of Susan's lifespan. Susan's family wanted Stewart to remember what he had done.

Stewart was relieved at first, but he soon grew weary of the ritual. Then it got worse. He found himself becoming depressed as he was reminded each Friday that he was responsible for a young woman's death. Writing her name on the check became more and more painful, and he stopped writing them.

The family went back to court to force him to continue. Four times during the next eight years, Stewart stopped paying and was forced to start again by court order. Finally, testifying that he was "haunted by Susan's death and tormented by the payments," Stewart went to court himself to appeal the "cruel" punishment that had been levied on him. In court he offered Susan's family two boxes of checks covering payments for the remainder of the eighteen years, plus an extra year. The family refused. "What we want," they said, "is to receive that check every week on time. We will pursue this until those years are completed, and we'll go back to court every month if we have to" (paraphrase).[1]

No matter how much he wanted to, Stewart could not escape his past. Week after week, year after year, he was reminded of the terrible deed he had committed, which brought so much shame and suffering to a family in this world and to himself.

What Stewart was experiencing represents what every man or woman encounters to some degree and in some way—the tyranny of valid guilt. That's our testimony until we discover what it means to be totally and completely forgiven.

We need the forgiveness of other people, but how much greater is our need to be forgiven by God Himself. After all, sin is essentially our violation of His character and of His commands. Every person reading this book has been sinning from childhood, and some of those sins have been especially cruel, hurtful, damaging, and shameful. We could never count the number of sins we've committed in our lifetimes, and we can never understand the depths of the sinful nature we've inherited from Adam. We cannot undo the past or reverse our actions, so without true and permanent pardon we're doomed to forever live behind the bars of a guilty soul.

People can't live that way and still be happy in life. That's why one of my most frequently asked questions is, "How can I find forgiveness?"

So far in this book, we've looked at the subject of assurance from the epistle of 1 John; at the subject of temptation from 1 Corinthians 13; and we've also found that Jesus' primary teaching about overcoming worry is in Matthew 6. Where, then, in the Bible can we find a much-needed passage on God's forgiveness? I could quote many verses to you from Scripture—we'll look at some of them in this chapter—but there's one passage that's especially powerful. You will recall this event in the life of David . . .

"Then Nathan said to David, 'You *are* the man! Thus says the *Lord* God of Israel: "I anointed you king over Israel, and I delivered you from the hand of Saul. I gave you your master's house and your master's wives into your keeping, and gave you the house of Israel and Judah. And if *that had been* too little, I also would have given you much more! Why have you despised the commandment of the *Lord*, to do evil in His sight? You have killed Uriah the Hittite with the sword; you have taken his wife *to be* your wife, and have killed him with the sword of the people of Ammon. . . .""""

"David said to Nathan, 'I have sinned . . .'" (2 Samuel 12:7-9, 13).

King David tumbled into one of the most infamous failures in history when he lusted after a woman named Bathsheba, whom he saw bathing. His lusts led to immorality, his immorality to murder, and the murder to a disastrous cover-up. For over a year, David lived in the blackness of bitter shame and secret guilt. As we read this story in 2 Samuel 11 – 12, we see it was the prophet Nathan who finally managed to pierce David's heart with the words, "You *are* the man!" (2 Samuel 12:7) When Nathan explained the consequences of David's actions, the king's stubborn pride finally broke and he replied, "I have sinned against the Lord" (verse 13).

In Psalms 51 and 32, David expresses his remorse and repentance in the form of two penitential psalms on what it's like to seek and find forgiveness. Psalm 51 represented David's initial prayer of confession and repentance. In Psalm 32, David evidently looked back on the whole experience and left us with a record of what it truly means to discover the deep and liberating forgiveness of God. Psalm 32 gives us a powerful answer to the question, "How can I find forgiveness?"

As I've read and studied this Psalm, it seems to me there are four great truths we need to claim from it: The priority, power, process, and promise of forgiveness. Let's walk through a few of these verses and I'll show you how they unfold.

## The Priority of Forgiveness

Whenever we sin, nothing should come before seeking God's full forgiveness. It must be our first priority. In Psalm 32:3-4, David described what happened to him when he delayed seeking God's forgiveness: "When I kept silent, my bones grew old through my groaning all the day long. For day and night Your hand was heavy upon me; my vitality was turned into the drought of summer."

Notice how David described his initial response to his actions. He kept silent. He became spiritually paralyzed. Not only did he try to keep his sin from God; he confided in no one else. He was unable to talk with those closest to him. Sinful behavior imprisons us in a tomb of loneliness and silence. Our fellowship with others is barricaded, and our fellowship with God is obstructed. Psalm 66:18 tells us that if we regard iniquity in our heart, the Lord will not hear.

This was no small thing for David, a man who was described as being "after God's own heart," who kept counsel with God constantly on every subject, the man who had written Psalm 23. Nor is it a small thing for us. Verse 3 is as true for us as for David when it says, "When I kept silent, my bones grew old." The Hebrew word for *old* carries the idea of "wasting away." David's energy and strength were diminished. He became weak as he carried the burden of unforgiven sin. The weight in his soul began to wear out the strength of his body, sapping his enthusiasm, draining away his energy, and making him feel like a worn-out old man. "Day and night Your hand was heavy upon me," he recalled, "my vitality was turned into the drought of summer" (verse 4).

I don't know if you've ever lived through a terrible drought; we're facing a prolonged one here in California where I live. When you see a drought-stricken area, the grass has turned brown, the crops have withered up, the ground is hard as concrete, the air as dry as dust, and the whole place looks like Death Valley. Without water everything wilts, withers, and wastes away. That's what happened to David's heart when the rivers of the Holy Spirit were shut off by the scorching nature of his sin.

One commentator explained, "Unrepentance and unforgiveness bring depression, emotional pain, alienation from God, and physical weakness. . . . Untold millions live in this condition; they even accept it as normal or inevitable. . . . I have had the experience of laboring under unforgiveness. At one time I was so depressed that I had stomach pains that would not go away. . . . Finally I went to the hospital, but there was no treatment. I needed to experience forgiveness—only in Christ did I find lasting relief—and I needed to forgive myself for participation in the pain that was mine."[2] Have you ever felt that way? Do you feel a drought in your heart now? Then you know God's pardon is priority.

You may remember the terrible wildfires that ravaged Colorado a few years ago. After much investigation, authorities discovered the fires had been started by an employee of the U.S. Forest Service who was suffering from a broken marriage. Her estranged husband wrote her a letter; and in her anger and hurt, she burned it in a campfire. Sparks from that fire spread out of control so quickly that before it was all over, nearly 140,000 acres were destroyed, along with 132 homes and the forced evacuation of thousands. She was arrested for arson, convicted, sent to prison, and fined more than $42 million.

When a reporter visited her behind bars, what she wanted to talk about was her need for forgiveness. "I can't give them back what they lost," she said. "I know how it feels because I lost, too. All I can say is I'm sorry. I know it's a healing process for them as it is for me. I just hope and pray they can forgive me. To live without forgiveness is a miserable thing."[3]

After his conviction for animal abuse, NFL football superstar Michael Vick made this comment in an interview with CBS News: "The first day I walked into prison, and he slammed that door, I knew the magnitude of the decision that I made, and the poor judgment, and what I allowed to happen to the animals. And, you know, it's no way of explaining the hurt and the guilt that I felt. And that was the reason I cried so many nights. . . . I blame me."[4]

That's the essence of these verses in Psalm 32. To live without forgiveness is miserable. When we do things that are harmful to God, to ourselves, and to other people, we feel badly about it. Sin creates guilt, guilt creates shame, and shame damages the way we view ourselves. It's a miserable thing to live in that endless cycle of sin, guilt, shame, and lowered self-esteem. It makes our bones grow old. It turns our vitality into the drought of summer. Yet, sadly, that's the way most people live. Furthermore, without the ultimate and eternal forgiveness of Christ, our metaphorical hell will one day be a real one. That's why being right with God through Jesus Christ—forgiven, pardoned, cleansed—is of the highest priority. God gave His very Son to make this possible, and Jesus shed His blood to accomplish it on our behalf.

## The Power of Forgiveness

That brings us to the subject of the power of forgiveness. Would you be free from your burden of guilt? There is power in the blood of Christ. Divine forgiveness is a powerful force, as the psalmist described it here in Psalm 32. Though this Psalm is the result of a broken, contrite, repentant heart, it begins with one of the Bible's happiest words—"Blessed!" If you're struggling with a guilty conscience, you may be wondering if you'll ever feel happy or blessed again. After all, some sins have catastrophic effects on our lives, and even the "smallest" ones are capable of separating us from the holiness of our perfect God. But the power of God's forgiveness can bring blessing back into your heart, like the hymn that says:

> *"O the deep, deep love of Jesus,*
> *vast, unmeasured, boundless, free!*
> *. . . and it lifts me up to glory,*
> *for it lifts me up to Thee!"*[5]

We get a glimpse into the power of God's forgiveness by noticing four different words David used to describe his sin in Psalm 32:1-2: "Blessed is he whose *transgression* is forgiven, whose *sin* is covered. Blessed is the man to whom the Lord does not impute *iniquity*, and in whose spirit there is no *deceit*." Notice the twofold use of the word blessing and the fourfold description of the sins from which we can be forgiven.

- *Transgression* describes defiant disobedience against God.

- *Sin* means to "miss the mark," based on a word for an archer who shoots an arrow but misses the target.

- *Iniquity* implies perversion, a distortion of what is right, something that is warped or twisted.

- *Deceit*, both in Hebrew and in English, carries the idea of deception, including self-deception.

In some ways, these four words describe the progression of David's sin. He disobeyed God's laws about sexual purity; the intents of his heart flew wild and missed the mark; his life became distorted and perverse; and he tried to cover it up, deceiving himself as well as others.

Yet the entire chain of rusted evil was instantly and totally broken and banished by God's grace at the moment of true repentance. One commentator said, "The psalmist declares that the forgiveness of sin of whatever kind— whether against God or human beings, whether great or small, whether conscientious or inadvertent, or whether by omission or commission—is to be found in God. The nature of the sin is not as important here as the blessedness of forgiveness!"[6]

The Bible uses many terms and metaphors to describe God's forgiveness. In the verses I've just quoted, David said that God forgave and covered his sin and did not impute iniquity to his account. Isaiah 55:7 uses the wonderful phrase, "He will abundantly pardon." Acts 10:43 talks about the remission of sin. Colossians 2:13-14 says, "Having forgiven you all trespasses, having wiped out the handwriting of requirements that was against us . . . having nailed it to the cross." Isaiah 43:25 says our sins are blotted out.

If you're struggling with being forgiven or with feeling forgiven, let me suggest you investigate this subject in the Bible. Using an online concordance or the cross-references of a study Bible, look up every verse you can find about God's forgiveness and make a list of the truths that speak most to you. Memorize some of the verses and quote them when the devil accuses your heart.

Let me tell you about a woman who did just that. Her name was Rosalind Goforth, and she was a well-known missionary to China. She and her husband, Jonathan, enjoyed an illustrious career in Asia for many years. But Rosalind encountered an interval in her life when she felt oppressed by a burden of sin. She felt guilty and dirty, and she nursed an inward sense of spiritual failure. Finally one evening when all was quiet, she settled at her desk with her Bible and concordance, determined to find out God's attitude toward the failures, the faults, the sins of His children. She put these words at the top of the page: "What God Does With Our Sins." As she searched the Scriptures, she compiled this list of seventeen truths:

1. He lays them on His Son, Jesus Christ. (Isaiah 53:6)

2. Christ takes them away. (John 1:29)

3. They are removed an immeasurable distance, as far as east is from west. (Psalm 103:12)

4. When sought for they are not found. (Jeremiah 50:20)

5. The Lord forgives them. (Ephesians 1:7)

6. He cleanses them all away by the blood of His Son. (1 John 1:7)

7. He cleanses them as white as snow or wool. (Isaiah 1:18; Psalm 51:7)

8. He abundantly pardons them. (Isaiah 55:7)

9. He tramples them under foot. (Micah 7:19, RSV)

10. He remembers them no more. (Hebrews 10:17)

11. He casts them behind His back. (Isaiah 38:17)

12. He casts them into the depths of the sea. (Micah 7:19)

13. He will not impute us with sins. (Romans 4:8)

14. He covers them. (Romans 4:7)

15. He blots them out. (Isaiah 43:25)

16. He blots them out as a thick cloud. (Isaiah 44:22)

17. He blots out even the proof against us, nailing it
    to His Son's Cross. (Colossians 2:14)[7]

Rosalind's feelings of oppression and shame couldn't withstand the onslaught of biblical truth, and the verses she found became flags of victory flying over her heart.

One verse is particularly intriguing on that list. Hebrews 10:17 says, "Their sins and their lawless deeds I will remember no more." We often say that God forgives and forgets our sins, but is that true? How can God, who is all-knowing, forget anything? When we commit a sin against Him, it's a deed done in time and space. It is a historical event. It's something that really happened. If God were to forget an event in history, He would not be omniscient (all knowing); and if He isn't omniscient, how can He be God? How, then, can we say He has forgotten our sin?

I think the word *forgotten* is used here in a judicial sense. The passage in Hebrews 10 is describing the ministry of Jesus Christ as our Great High Priest. The sacrifice He made was a once-for-all sacrifice. Because of His blood, God expunges the record of our sins. No other sacrifice is ever again needed. There is no more record of our sins on heaven's books, not a dash, not a comma, not a smudge. Although God is omniscient and knows everything that has ever happened or will ever happen, He will never again view us with that sin in mind. It's as though it never occurred.

That's the power of His forgiveness. That's the power of the blood of Christ.

Isaiah 64:6 says that without God's forgiveness, we're dressed in "filthy rags." We're caked with mud and filth. After His forgiveness, we're clothed in the righteousness of Christ. According to Colossians 3 and 4, becoming a Christian means that we "put off the old man with his deeds," such as anger, wrath, malice, blasphemy, filthy language, and lying. We clothe ourselves in "the new man who is renewed in knowledge according to the image of Christ." Take a moment and imagine being covered with mud, mire, grime, and filth. Now think of hot showers and fresh clothes. That's a picture of how it feels to put on the new man. That's what it means to be a forgiven follower of the Lord Jesus Christ.

## The Process of Forgiveness

How, then, do we claim and appropriate this forgiveness into our own experience? The process is revealed in Psalm 32:5, when David wrote, "I acknowledged my sin to You, and my iniquity I have not hidden. I said, 'I will confess my transgressions to the Lord,' and You forgave the iniquity of my sin."

Confession is all about naked honesty before God. David came to realize how he had lusted after Bathsheba, taken advantage of his royal position, committed immorality, arranged for a husband to die in battle, married the woman with whom he had slept, and tried to cover up the whole sordid affair. He had sinned against Bathsheba, against Uriah, against his own family, and against his army and nation. But primarily his sin was against God since God was the one who established the rules concerning morality and murder and honesty and ethics. David broke several of God's Ten Commandments— rules that summarize and stream from the holy character of a perfect God. While David had hurt many people, it was the laws of God he had broken.

His confession, then, had to be first of all directed above, to the Lord. At the root of every sin, from the pettiest offense to the most heinous act, there is a disregard for the character and standards of an all-powerful God whose holiness establishes the moral baseline of the universe. Sin is an insult to the One who created us and who sustains us every moment of our lives. Before the sin claims any victims, it has already been an injury to the person of God.

If you sin against me I can forgive you personally, but I can't give you a deeper level of forgiveness with God. I can't remove the offense against the Lord. Only He can do that. The world wants to dismiss the category of sin altogether; but just as we cannot find healing until we admit a sickness is real, so we can't find forgiveness if we deny the reality of sin.

The Bible says, "If we confess our sins, He is faithful and just to forgive us our sins and to cleanse us from all unrighteousness" (1 John 1:9). To find forgiveness, we have to do what David did—acknowledge our sin before God in earnest prayer, tell Him we are sorry, ask His forgiveness, tell Him that by His help we are willing to turn from our sin, and then trust Him to be faithful and just to forgive our sin and to cleanse us from all unrighteousness.

When you come to Him in contrite confession, you can trust Him to nail your sins to the cross of Christ, to cover them with His blood, to blot them out of His book, to abundantly pardon, to wash you whiter than snow, to cast your sins behind His back, to cast them into the depths of the sea, to blot them out, to remove them as far as the east is from the west, and to remember them no more. Then you can sing, as Charles Wesley wrote in his great hymn, "O for a Thousand Tongues to Sing":

> *He breaks the power of cancelled sin,*
> *He sets the prisoner free;*
> *His blood can make the foulest clean,*
> *His blood availed for me.*

## The Promise of Forgiveness

God has promised to forgive the contrite heart; and when our sins are forgiven, the barriers are shattered between us and our God. The wall separating us from His fellowship is lowered. The veil is torn in two, allowing us access into our Father's presence. We have fellowship with Him; and that's why Psalm 32, though written against such a sordid backdrop, begins and ends on such high notes. The first verse says, "Blessed is he whose transgression is forgiven," and the last verse of Psalm 32 says, "Be glad in the Lord and rejoice, you righteous; and shout for joy, all you upright in heart!"

Because of God's forgiveness, we are declared righteous and upright in heart, and that's something to shout about. He sent His Son to die for us and to rise again. Romans 4:25 says Christ "was delivered up because of our offenses, and was raised because of our justification." His message to you is, "Having forgiven you because of the blood of My Son, I no longer regard your guilt and I don't want you to regard it either. I want you to live in a new way with Me, to walk with Me in a fellowship so rich that it will overflow and overcome your old sinful tendencies."

> *"There is unspeakable joy . . . for the person who knows release from guilt and the relief of forgiveness."[8]*
> ~ STUART BRISCOE

The word *blessed* in verse 1 is, in some ways, similar to our word *happy*. It means much more than "happy," but it includes the ideas of happiness, cheerfulness, and joy. Happy are those whose sin is forgiven! Shout for joy!

This truth is so incredible and revolutionary that your life is bound to be changed forever if you will only grasp it. When God forgives us, He welcomes us into His presence where there "is fullness of joy" and "pleasures forevermore" (Psalm 16:11). David's words about forgiveness appear in what many people would call the Hymnbook of the Hebrews, the book of Psalms. It's a reminder to us to sing together with great joy when we gather for worship. We can sing because we're happy; we can sing because we're free.

That said, I have to make an additional point right now. In David's case, his sin was forgiven, but not all the consequences of his sin were reversed. We have to be honest about this. Terrible problems arose in David's life and in his kingship as a result of the chain reaction of his foolishness. Sometimes our wounds heal, but there are scars that remain. We have to face the fact that God's forgiveness doesn't instantly remove all the results of our sinful behavior. But even in this, the Lord will get the glory.

Believe it or not, David and Bathsheba ended up bearing a child who became an ancestor of the Messiah. Matthew 1:6, giving us the lineage of Christ, says, "Jesse begot David the king. David the king begot Solomon by her who had been the wife of Uriah." The sin was forgiven; some of the consequences had to be dealt with; but in the end God used it all in ways that reflected the mysterious depths of His mercy. When Romans 8:28 says that "all things work together for good to those who love God," it means that somehow in His grace the Lord can even bring good out of forgiven sin.

Since God has forgiven us, then, we must accept His forgiveness. Periodically, I hear people say, "Well, I know God has forgiven me, and my wife has forgiven me or my husband has forgiven me, but I cannot forgive myself." I understand that feeling, but think of it this way: We aren't called to forgive ourselves. Our job is to confess our sin and receive God's forgiveness. His job is to forgive us and cleanse us from our unrighteousness. Forgiveness is something that occurs between two parties. Trying to forgive yourself would be like trying to shake your own hand. Our responsibility is to accept the forgiveness God has already granted.

We're also to forgive others for their sins against us. Ephesians 4:32 says, "Be kind to one another, tenderhearted, forgiving one another, even as God in Christ forgave you." Colossians 3:12-13 adds, "Therefore, as the elect of God, holy and beloved, put on tender mercies, kindness, humility, meekness, longsuffering; bearing with one another, and forgiving one another, if anyone has a complaint against another; even as Christ forgave you, so you also must do."

When we forgive someone who has wronged us we set them free and we also set ourselves free. Bitterness of our own hearts is like a poison that continually eats away at our joy and happiness. When we forgive those whom God has forgiven, it's liberating for them, for us, and for the Church of the Lord Jesus.

One of the best illustrations of this comes from missionary Ruby Scott in her autobiography, *Jungle Harvest*. She was a Bible translator in an isolated tribe in the jungles of southern Mexico. She worked in a village called Chivalito and helped establish a church there. Among the converts was a man named Rosendo, who was the former village drunk. Having come to Christ, he grew to be a hard-working, faithful family man who actively served the Lord. He was the president or leader of the congregation. His testimony was an inspiration to the village and he was active in sharing his faith with others.

The growth of the church was a threat to the local witch doctor, a man named Lencho. He was reported to be the most powerful witch doctor in the area, and he openly vowed to destroy the growing Christian testimony in the village of Chivalito. The church knew a satanic attack was coming, so they memorized verses that emphasized the power and authority of Jesus Christ. Meanwhile, the witch doctor was planning an elaborate trap for Rosendo. The whole story is too complicated and lengthy to fully relate, but the long and short of the story is that Rosendo, having been previously enslaved by alcohol, was lured into a carefully-planned web in which he found himself on a wild drinking spree with his superiors and supervisors. He had a very public and embarrassing relapse. The whole village was startled to see him stagger down the street, with the witch doctor beside him, making fun of Rosendo and making the Christians the laughingstock of town.

> *"You choose whether to live in the freedom of forgiveness or in the bitterness of bondage."*[9]
> ~ ELMER TOWNS

On Sunday the church gathered in a somber mood. Every believer had been laughed at that week. They tried singing a few hymns, but then, to everyone's surprise, Rosendo appeared from the jungle path and stepped into the building. All eyes were on him as the congregational hymn ended. He motioned that he wanted to speak.

Rosendo stood up, his eyes focused on the ground, and in a clear, concise way he explained what had happened. He gave the full story but did not minimize what he had done or try to excuse himself. When he finished, he quoted 1 John

1:9: "If we confess our sins, He is faithful and just to forgive us our sins and to cleanse us from all unrighteousness."

He told the silenced crowd that he had sinned and brought ridicule on the church and on the name of the Lord Himself. He said he had earnestly confessed his sin to the Lord and sought forgiveness. He ended by saying, "I have not only brought shame to our Lord, but to you too. All of you have been ridiculed and taunted because of what I did. I'm sorry. I don't know if you want to forgive me or not."

He sat down and put his face in his hands, and there was silence for a few moments. Then a man named Felix stood up and asked a question that seemed out of place. He said, "Remember a few weeks ago when it rained three days without letting up? That rain left a huge mud puddle in our front yard. Several times [my son] Elpidio dashed out the door to play in the muddy water. 'Elpidio,' I called him, 'get away from that mud.' But after several attempts, he finally made his way to the puddle. Suddenly I heard an awful splat and a cry. Elpidio was face down in the mud.

"Now friends," Felix continued, "What do you think I said? Do you think I just stood there rubbing my hands together and said, 'Well, I told you. Now it's your problem!' No, of course not. Elpidio is my little son and I love him. I hurried to him, picked him up, wiped the mud from his face, and held him until he quit crying.

"Friends, our brother Rosendo has fallen on his face in the mud. We have a Heavenly Father who loves him, has helped him up, and wiped the mud off him. He will hold him close and love him until the pain and embarrassment goes away. All of us have felt the splat of Rosendo's fall. We have been laughed at, and it hurt. But our Lord suffered a much deeper hurt for the things we have done than we will ever suffer because of what Rosendo did. Rosendo has confessed his sin, and the Lord has forgiven him. Now he is asking us to forgive him, too."

Felix paused for a long minute and looked around as if thinking about what to do. Then in a quiet voice he said, "Let's take a vote. All who want to forgive Rosendo and pray for him, put up your hand." A moment later, Felix stepped over and touched Rosendo's shoulder and whispered to him. Looking up, Rosendo saw that the whole room had become a sea of hands. Another member stood up quietly and began singing "How Great Thou Art" and the whole congregation sang:

*And when I think that God, His Son not sparing,*
*Sent Him to die, I scarce can take it in,*
*That on the cross, my burden gladly bearing,*
*He bled and died to take away my sin.* [10]

The church in the village of Chivalito grew to capacity, the Gospel spread, the Scriptures were translated, and many souls came into the kingdom. Out of forgiven sin came a new intense desire for holiness and evangelism. [11]

Don't continue to anguish over shortcomings that God has forgiven. Don't keep trying to please Him by perfunctory and fearful obedience to the Law. Accept the forgiveness He offers, enjoy the grace He gives, and stand fast in the liberty by which Christ has made us free. In that way, we can be "more than conquerors" in every area and arena of life.

Without Christ, our world is a culture of fear. Without His forgiveness, we're in danger of guilt. Without His pardon, we're in danger of judgment. Without His life, we're in danger of death. Without His promises, we're in danger of chaos. Without His presence, we're in danger of loneliness. Without His Gospel, we're in danger of despair. Without His blood, we're in danger of hell. But God demonstrated His own love for us in that while we were yet sinners Christ died for us (Romans 5:8). He died for all, that those who live should live no longer for themselves, but for Him who died for them and rose again. God was, in Christ, reconciling the world to Himself. He made Him who knew no sin to be sin for us, that we might become the righteousness of God in Him (2 Corinthians 5:15, 19, 21).

There is forgiveness with God, for the grace of God knows no limits. Blessed are those whose transgression is forgiven, whose sin is covered. Blessed are those to whom the Lord does not impute iniquity. Be glad in the Lord and rejoice. Shout for joy, you upright in heart.

> *"There is a fountain filled with blood*
> *drawn from Emmanuel's veins;*
> *And sinners plunged beneath that flood*
> *lose all their guilty stains."*[12]
> ~ WILLIAM COWPER, IN HIS HYMN
> "THERE IS A FOUNTAIN FILLED WITH BLOOD"

# QUESTIONS TO DISCUSS

**1.** How would you define the word *sin*?

_____

_____

_____

_____

_____

_____

**2.** In a group discussion you don't necessarily have to be specific, but in general terms can you identify with David in Psalm 32? Can you think of a time in your life when you might have written something expressing the sentiments he shared in this Psalm?

_____

_____

_____

_____

_____

_____

**3.** In the story of David and Bathsheba, the prophet Nathan was used to bring David to his senses. Has anyone ever helped you see a crucial error in your life? Do you know of a time when someone's admonishment led to another person's sincere confession of sin?

_____

_____

_____

_____

_____

_____

_____

**4.** In the story of missionary Rosalind Goforth, which of the images that she found in the Bible is the most vivid to you? Why?

_____

_____

_____

_____

_____

_____

_____

**5.** If God has forgiven us of the deepest sins imaginable, why do you think we have so much trouble forgiving others? Is there someone you need to forgive?

_____

_____

_____

_____

_____

**6.** Do you believe self-forgiveness is possible? What would you say to someone who said, "I just can't forgive myself"?

_____

_____

_____

_____

_____

_____

*"Forgiveness is the key which unlocks the door of resentment and the handcuffs of hatred. It breaks the chains of bitterness and the shackles of selfishness. The forgiveness of Jesus not only takes away our sins but it also makes them as if they had never been. That is the way we must forgive. The Holy Spirit makes us able to do it through the love of God which He brings into our hearts."*[13]

~ Corrie ten Boom

# CHAPTER FIVE

# Is There Only One Way to God?

LEE STROBEL WAS AN ATHEISTIC JOURNALIST who, after poring over the evidence for the truthfulness of Christianity, became a follower of Jesus Christ and began applying his investigative journalism to the defense of the faith.[1] Today his "Case" books (like *The Case for Faith* and *The Case for a Creator*) are best sellers. Lee readily admits that before his conversion, he disliked one verse of Scripture more than any other—John 14:6, where Jesus said, "I am the way, the truth, and the life. No one comes to the Father except through Me."

"This was the statement I found most offensive," Strobel wrote of his pre-conversion view of this verse. "It's one thing to claim to be *a* way to God—but *the* way? That sounds pretty intolerant!"[2] Strobel feels differently now, for, having come to Christ and grown in his understanding of truth, he teaches that John 14:6 is one of the greatest statements of one of our greatest doctrines.

Yet John 14:6 is an example of what Strobel calls "fighting words." In his book, *The Case for Christ*, Strobel told the story of Walter Chaplinsky, who, in 1940, "caused a ruckus in Rochester, New Hampshire, by loudly denouncing organized religion as being 'a racket' and condemning several Christian denominations by name. The result: he found himself arrested and convicted under a state law making it a crime to speak 'any offensive, derisive or annoying word to any person who is lawfully in any street or other public place.'

"Believing that his free-speech rights were being violated," Strobel recounts, "Chaplinsky appealed his case all the way to the United States Supreme Court. However, in 1942 the justices unanimously affirmed his conviction, saying that 'fighting words' like the ones he shouted fall outside the protection of the First Amendment. Thirty years later, the high court clarified its definition of 'fighting words' by calling them 'personally abusive epithets' that are 'inherently likely to provoke violent action.'"[3]

Since 1942, the phrase "fighting words" has been part of the American vocabulary and a part of our legal definitions. Everyone knows that all words are not equal; some are more inflammatory or provocative than others.

When it comes to the teachings of Jesus, all of His words are inspired, unbreakable, authoritative, and life changing. Yet much of our society embraces some of His teaching while rejecting the rest. When Jesus told us to love one another, that's widely accepted as good advice even by secularists. Ethicists respect His Golden Rule. His words about the lilies of the field and the birds of the air, as we studied in a prior chapter, are deeply meaningful to most who read them. Even nonbelievers can meditate on soothing statements like, "Let not your heart be troubled" (John 14:1).

But when Jesus claimed to be the only way to God, well, those are "fighting words" as far as today's world is concerned. John 14:6 is a bridge too far for post-modern, open-minded, politically correct pundits. In our age of so-called tolerance, this has arguably become the most unpopular statement from the lips of Jesus.

Steve McSwain is a popular speaker and author in liberal circles and an ambassador to the Council for a Parliament of the World's Religions. He recently wrote in the *Huffington Post* that people ask him all the time if he believes Jesus is the only way to God. His answer is: "He is my way to God . . . Is He the only way? I do not think so. And do not bother to point to John 14:6 as a 'proof text' that Jesus himself said He was the 'only way to God.' John 14:6 may be the most abused and misused verse of Scripture in the 21st century."

McSwain didn't offer an alternate interpretation in his column or suggest how the Lord's clearly spoken words in John 14:6 might be explained away. He simply ridiculed those who believe in John 14:6 as "nervous, frightened Christians" with "little faith" who "feel they are under attack" and "cannot tolerate a difference of opinion."[4]

That's the majority view in today's society. Oprah Winfrey, for example, said, "One of the biggest mistakes humans make is to believe there is only one way. Actually, there are many diverse paths leading to what you call God."[5]

Popular Jewish rabbi and television host Shmuley Boteach shares a similar conviction. "I am absolutely against any religion that says that one faith is superior to another," he said. "I don't see how that is anything different than spiritual racism. It's a way of saying that we are closer to God than you, and that's what leads to hatred."[6]

In his book, *The Case for Faith*, Lee Strobel wrote, "Many people consider it arrogant, narrow-minded, and bigoted for Christians to contend that the only path to God must go through Jesus of Nazareth. In a day of religious pluralism and tolerance, this exclusivity claim is politically incorrect, a verbal slap in the face of other belief systems . . . When I was an atheist, I bristled at assertions by Christians that they held a monopoly on the only correct approach to Christianity. 'Who do they think they are?' I'd grouse."[7]

Jesus' claim of exclusivity is one of the biggest obstacles many people face when considering Christianity. In our age of pluralism and "tolerance," the question "Is there only one way to God?" is perhaps the most volatile question we could ask or be asked.

It won't surprise you that I love the fourteenth chapter of John, and I especially treasure verse 6. What others label as intolerant, I label as invaluable, gracious, and glorious. This is a verse I'll never give up because it is so truthful and so hopeful. It's the essence of the Good News, and we have no intention of being on the defensive about that. John 14:6 is a verse to memorize, ponder, treasure, and share with a needy world. I can't be responsible for how others respond or react to it, but I can hold it out as bread for the hungry and water for the thirsty.

Let's begin by looking at the setting. On the night of His arrest, Jesus gathered His disciples around Him in an upper room, eating and drinking with them and giving them His final set of teachings prior to His death. He spoke to them about a number of troubling things that would soon take place. He then comforted them with these timeless words: "Let not your heart be troubled; you believe in God, believe also in Me. In My Father's house are many mansions; if it were not so, I would have told you. I go to prepare a place for you. And if I go and prepare a place for you, I will come again and receive you to Myself; that where I am, there you may be also. And where I go you know, and the way you know."

When Jesus told His disciples that the way to God was certain and knowable, Thomas responded with a question of perplexity. This was in keeping with what we know of Thomas' personality. If he had been an American, he would have been from Missouri, the "Show Me" state. He was skeptical until fully convinced; but once convinced, Thomas was dauntless. On this occasion, he said to Christ, "Lord, we do not know where You are going, and how can we know the way?"

Thomas had missed our Lord's point in the earlier verses. Jesus was talking about going to heaven to prepare for us. At the end of the age, Jesus said, He would return and take us to be with Him there forever. Thomas evidently thought Jesus was announcing that He was going to take a trip to a hidden location, perhaps a secure spot within the boundaries of Israel or the eastern Mediterranean region. Thomas wanted to know how the disciples could find the way and rejoin their Lord. He wanted an earthly map to the Lord's retreat site.

Well, I'm glad Thomas misunderstood and I'm glad he asked his question, because it occasioned a wonderful response. When Thomas asked, "How can we know the way?" Jesus said simply, "I am the way, the truth, and the life. No one comes to the Father except through Me."

It was a simple answer, but those simple words contain the kernels of infinite truth. In His powerful statement Jesus declared Himself to be the answer to the three greatest questions of the human heart.

- How can I be saved? Jesus is the way.

- How can I be sure? Jesus is the truth.

- How can I be satisfied? Jesus is the life.[8]

In order to understand what Jesus was saying, we need to take our minds all the way back to the Garden of Eden. Before Adam sinned, he enjoyed three very special privileges with God his Creator:

- He communed with God intimately; we see him walking with God.

- He knew God in reality; we see him believing what God said.

- He possessed spiritual life fully; we see him living in paradise.

But when Adam fell in rebellion against God, he lost all three of his special privileges with God. His communion was broken; he hid from God. His knowledge was corrupted; he believed Satan's lies. His life was shattered; he was beginning to die.

John 14:6 reverses those three tragic realities. Our present condition apart from God is a mirror of Adam and Eve's condition after the Fall. We are alienated from God. We don't have fellowship with Him. We are ignorant of the truth of God. We cannot comprehend God in reality. And we are condemned to physical and spiritual death. Everything that Adam lost in the Fall is exactly the state of condemned humanity today without Jesus Christ.

That's why we call the Gospel the Good News. In Christ, we can recover everything lost in the Fall. In Jesus Christ, instead of

> *"The early followers of Jesus were so convinced that Jesus was the only way to Heaven that they didn't even call themselves Christians . . . they called themselves, 'followers of the Way'"*
> *(Acts 9:1, 2; 22:4; 24:14).*
> ~ STEVEN JAMES[9]

alienation from God, we can have fellowship with Him. Instead of ignorance of God's ways, we can know His truth. And instead of death, we can know life in Him.

The way, the truth, and the life! Jesus is communion restored. Jesus is truth recovered. Jesus is life regained—the full and permanent reversal of Genesis 3.

That's the meaning of John 14:6. Now, let's look at it phrase by phrase.

## Jesus Is Communion Restored

The first phrase in verse 6 says, "I am the way." Apart from Christ, we cannot have communion with God because of the impenetrable barrier of sin, but Jesus came to remove that barrier. The apostle Paul said it this way: "For there is one God and one Mediator between God and men, the Man Christ Jesus" (1 Timothy 2:5). I like the way *The Living Bible* renders this verse: "God is on one side and all the people on the other side, and Christ Jesus, Himself a man, is between them to bring them together."

That's what we mean when we say Jesus is the Mediator. The book of Hebrews calls this "a new and living way which He consecrated for us, through the veil, that is, His flesh" (Hebrews 10:20).

Jesus is certainly the teacher of the way. He is the guide along the way and the provider of the way, but He is more than that. He *is* the way. He *is* the way to restored communion with the heavenly Father.

I need that. I have trouble finding the way, even in a geographical sense around town. In driving, I'm directionally challenged. I spend at least a few minutes every week totally lost. Once, when I was pastoring a church in Fort Wayne, Indiana, I was conducting a funeral and driving behind the hearse to the grave site. I was busy talking to a friend about a particular church, and I absentmindedly turned onto another street and drove to that church. The hearse went on to the cemetery, of course, but I didn't know where to go. You can imagine how embarrassed I felt when I showed up late to conduct the graveside service.

Now suppose I was in an unfamiliar city and I needed directions. I might approach a person who would say, "Well, Pastor Jeremiah, turn left, then right, then left, and go several blocks, then turn left again." In that case, I'd probably be lost all afternoon. I wouldn't be able to keep those directions in my mind; and if he wrote them down, I'm not sure I could follow them.

But what if the man said, "Oh, Pastor Jeremiah, I know exactly where you need to go. Let me be the way. I will take you there." That would be a different matter. And that's what Jesus is talking about here. Jesus not only points out the way, He *is* the way. He is the pathway personified. He became the directions. He Himself is my way of restored communion and fellowship with God.

## Jesus Is Truth Recovered

The next phrase in John 14:6 says, "I am . . . the truth." Jesus is utterly dependable and trustworthy. You can take Him at His word. When we meet Him, we move from the false to the true, from deception to reality, from relative confusion to absolute knowledge. Throughout his Gospel, the apostle John stressed Jesus as the Truth.

- "And the Word became flesh and dwelt among us, and we beheld His glory, the glory as of the only begotten of the Father, full of grace and truth."—JOHN 1:14

- "For the law was given through Moses, but grace and truth came through Jesus Christ." —JOHN 1:17

- "You shall know the truth, and the truth shall make you free."—JOHN 8:32

- "I tell you the truth."—JOHN 8:46

- "Sanctify them by Your truth. Your word is truth."—JOHN 17:17

- "For this cause I was born, and for this cause I have come into the world, that I should bear witness to the truth."—JOHN 18:37

The Bible teaches that Jesus Christ was and is the conveyor of truth. But that's not all. He's not just the communicator of truth, the witness to the truth, the origin of the truth, or the preacher of the truth. He *is* the Truth embodied. Christ is the final revelation of God to man. He is the true picture of God to man. Truth is not a system or a philosophy; it's a Person. If you want to know the truth of God, you must come to know Christ because He alone is truth. When you seek Him, you will find the one true and living God.

The truth is not a relative thing; it has a certain inflexibility and intolerance to it. That's its nature. I'm not just speaking in philosophical or theological terms. This is true mathematically and scientifically.

John Phillips put it this way: "Truth is always exclusive, always dogmatic, always intolerant of non-truth. Otherwise it would not be truth eternal, and absolute. It makes no difference whether the truth is a mathematical truth, a scientific truth, or, as here, a spiritual truth . . . For instance: 'Two multiplied by two equals four.' That is a narrow, dogmatic, intolerant statement. Error says, 'Two multiplied by two is three.' Truth cannot accept that kind of 'tolerance.' Since Jesus is the truth, He excludes all error, no matter how popular, widespread, ancient, or convincing it may be."[10]

Dave Hunt made the observation, "Everyone knows that to fly an airplane or practice medicine or even bake a cake one must follow specific procedures. One can't even play a game without rules. Then why attempt to avoid the rules which God has set in the realm of the spirit? Sincerity won't get astronauts to the moon, nor will it prevent arsenic from killing the person who ingested it by mistake. Yoga won't even pay a traffic ticket. It makes no sense to set out from Los Angeles to New York without a map. What folly it would be to refuse to follow a map because maps are so restrictive, and to insist that any road in any direction will do! How much greater is the folly of insisting that any road sincerely followed will take one to heaven!"[11]

In *Discipleship Journal*, author Mack Stiles tells how he led a young man from Sweden named Andreas to Christ. One part of their conversation is especially instructive:

Andreas said, "I've been told if I decide to follow Jesus, He will meet my needs and my life will get very good."

"No, Andreas, no!" said Stiles.

Andreas blinked with surprise.

"Actually, Andreas, you may accept Jesus and find that life goes very badly for you."

"What do you mean?" he asked.

"Well, you may find that your friends reject you, you could lose your job, your family might oppose your decision. There are a lot of bad things that may happen to you if you decide to follow Jesus. Andreas, when Jesus calls you, He calls you to go the way of the cross."

"Then why would I want to follow Jesus?"

The answer: "Andreas, because Jesus is true."[12]

I don't ever want to look back over my life and realize I had built it on a set of false assumptions. A lot of people construct assumptions that are broadminded and permissive. If it feels good, they do it. If it sounds good, they believe it. If it looks good, they want it.

But what if it's all a lie? What then?

Jesus is the way and the truth. He alone can restore our communion with God and bring us back to the glorious realities we need.

## Jesus Is Life Regained

Jesus is also the life. He is life incarnate, the opposite of death and darkness. *Life* is another of the great words that runs like a golden chain through the Gospel of John. It's a word that occurs more than forty times in the fourth Gospel, and it's often modified by the adjective *everlasting*.

- "In Him was life, and the life was the light of men."—JOHN 1:4

- "Whoever believes in Him should not perish but have everlasting life."—JOHN 3:16

- "The water I shall give him will become in him a fountain of water springing up into everlasting life."—JOHN 4:14

- "The Son gives life to whom He will."—JOHN 5:21

- "But you are not willing to come to Me that you may have life."—JOHN 5:40

- "I am the bread of life."—JOHN 6:35

I'm tempted to list all forty-one references to "life" in John's Gospel, but you get the idea. Christ is the one who has come to emancipate us from death. I'm not just talking about physical death. I'm talking about spiritual death, being dead to God and His truth. Many people talk about how alive they are. They're alive to themselves, to the world, to money, to pleasure, to excitement. But they're dead to God and have no relationship with Him. Jesus came to give us life and to give it eternally. As John 10:10 says, "I have come that they may have life, and that they may have it more abundantly."

In the story of the Prodigal Son in Luke 15, the father was overjoyed when his son returned from the far country. He said, "For this my son was dead and is alive again; he was lost and is found" (verse 24). When the boy was living in debauchery in a foreign land, he was inwardly dead. He was dead to his father and to his family. He was dead to everything that was good and alive in that house. He was dead spiritually and to God. But when he repented and came home, he became alive to his father, alive to his family, alive to all the pursuits that they enjoyed together, and alive to himself. He experienced an inward resurrection. The same thing happens to us when we come to Christ.

Paul told the Ephesians, "And you He made alive, who were dead in trespasses and sins" (Ephesians 2:1). Another passage in the New Testament speaks of passing from death to life (1 John 3:14).

Colossians 2:13 says, "He has made alive together with Him, having forgiven you all trespasses." And 2 Corinthians 5:17 says, "If anyone is in Christ, he is a new creation; old things have passed away; behold, all things have become new."

Jesus Christ didn't come into this world simply to invigorate our old sinful nature. He didn't come to just refine the ugliness in our life. He didn't come to put a new suit on a corpse. He came to raise us from the kingdom of death to the kingdom of life. I don't know of a better way to describe what happens to a person who accepts Jesus Christ than a kind of inward resurrection. We come alive and experience a relationship with God.

My friend Ravi Zacharias gave this testimony: "I have traveled the world. I have searched high and low. I have found nothing that satisfies my mind, my heart, and the deepest longings of my soul like Jesus does. He is not only the way, the truth, and the life; He is personal to me. He is *my* way, and *my* truth, and *my* life—just as He can be for anyone who reaches out to Him."[13]

Several years ago, I was speaking to some students at a university in New Jersey and there was a question and answer time at the end of my presentation. We hadn't been in the session for five minutes before a fellow in the back of the room raised his hand and said, "I've listened to what you said today, Reverend. I want to ask you a question. Do you believe Jesus Christ is the only way to God?"

I said to him: "Sir, it really doesn't make any difference what I think. It really doesn't make any difference what I believe. What really makes a difference is what God says and what Jesus says. I don't want you to go away from here thinking about what David Jeremiah believes. I want you to go away from here thinking about what God says in His Word. He says, 'I am the way, the truth, and the life. No man cometh unto the Father except through Me.'"

In this chapter, I've used one primary passage to answer the question, "Is there only one way to God?" But the truth of John 14:6 is echoed throughout the Bible. For example, Acts 4:12 says: "Nor is there salvation in any other, for there is no other name under heaven given among men by which we must be saved."

There is only one name by which we must be saved, and it's the name Jesus, a name that means literally, "Jehovah Saves." If there had been another way to redeem the human race, don't you think God would have chosen it? Somehow, in the mysterious, hidden spiritual laws that God built into the fabric of the universe, there is a principle that fallen humanity can be restored only by the sacrificial and voluntary death of an innocent and eternal Lamb. That law cannot be violated. You can't change it. You might disbelieve it, but you cannot alter it. If you try to climb up to heaven by some other way, you'll never get there. There is no other Savior, no other Redeemer, no other Jesus, no other Name.

Someone said: "Christianity is exclusive. It proclaims one ultimate problem of humanity (sin), one ultimate need of humanity (salvation), and one ultimate Savior for humanity (Jesus). It levels the playing field among all people by announcing that all are equally in need for the same Savior. But here's the kicker: Christianity's proclamation of exclusivity, *one Savior* for all people, is also its proclamation of inclusivity: one Savior *for all people* . . . Christianity, then, is [both] the most exclusive and most inclusive religion [because] Jesus is the exclusive savior who inclusively invites all people. It all hinges on Jesus."[14]

The New Testament scholar Bruce Milne wrote: "Jesus alone is the way to God, but he is the way for all, and so whatever the religious background of an individual, or lack of religion, Jesus in His grace welcomes every one of them to the Father if they will come through him. For them too he is ready to prepare a place in the Father's house."[15]

I want to proclaim this message to the world with boldness and intrepidity. But I also want to proclaim it to the Church. The vast majority of the people to whom I speak are Christians, and it seems to me this passage should motivate us like a lightning bolt. If Jesus truly is the only way to God, how do we explain our complacency? How do we explain our willingness to go uncaringly week after week, month after month, and year after year working alongside those who don't know Christ and living in neighborhoods filled with people who don't know God? It is so easy to try not to disturb anyone because they have their way and we have our way. But the Bible says there is only one way, and that is His way; and the world around you needs to know that way.

As Christians, we know that way and are ambassadors of that way. We must communicate that way to others. If Jesus Christ is the only way to God, would it not seem logical that those of us who have come to God through Christ would be fiery representatives of that truth to everyone we meet, going out of our way to share with them with a sense of urgency of finding Christ?

We have become such nice Christians. We never want to offend anyone. We want to dialogue with everybody and sit down and talk it all through. We'd rather not be offensive or risk rocking the boat. But when we get down to the bottom line, we're still at the same place—there is only one way to God, and that is through Christ.

If Jesus Christ is the only way to God, and we know that way, and there are people all around us who are lost and don't know that way, should we not be seeking by every means at our disposal to point them to that way?

Dr. N. T. Wright wrote of John 14:6, "Though . . . it's true that many Christians and churches have been arrogant in the way they have presented the gospel, the whole setting of this passage shows that such arrogance is a denial of the very truth it's claiming to present.

"The truth, the life, through which we know and find the way, is Jesus himself: the Jesus who washed the disciples' feet and told them to copy His example, the Jesus who was on His way to give His life as the shepherd for the sheep.

"Was that arrogant? Was that self-serving?"[16]

John Phillips takes us back to the original question of this chapter and leaves a picture in our minds with a story he told: "A pioneer missionary in Africa told how he was taking the gospel to a new tribe, far to the north. With his bearers, he arrived at a village, a point beyond which his porters refused to go. The missionary appealed to the local chief. Was there someone in his village who could act as his guide to the distant northern tribe? The chief summoned a man, tall, battle scarred, carrying a large axe. A bargain was made and the next morning the missionary set off through the bush, following his new guide.

"The way became increasingly rough and the path had all but disappeared. There was an occasional mark blazed on a tree, occasionally a narrow path. Finally the missionary called a halt. He asked the guide if he was sure he knew the way. The man pulled himself up to his full height. 'White man,' he said, 'You see this axe in my hand? You see these scars on my body? With this axe I blazed the trail to the tribal village to which we go. I came from there. These scars I received when I made the way. You ask me if I know the way? Before I came, there was no way. I am the way.'"[17]

I want you to know that the Lord Jesus has the scars on His body that He suffered while making a way for us through the barrier of sin. Before Him, there was no way. Without Jesus, we have no hope. Without Him, we are lost and can never know God on our own. But Jesus came and condescended to put Himself within the limitations of a human body. He lived righteously and perfectly for about thirty years in a place not much bigger than a postage stamp. He let Himself be beaten, jeered, and nailed to a piece of wood. With the cross, with the scars on His body, with His amazing grace, He forged the way. He is our way, our truth, and our life. John 14:6 is one of the central passages in the Word of God, and it gives us the answer to the question: Is there only one way to God?

The answer is yes. His name is Jesus Christ, and I recommend Him to you.

———◦———

# QUESTIONS TO DISCUSS

**1.** Have you had conversations with or do you know people who become agitated by the Christian truth of the exclusivity of Christ—that He is the only way of salvation? How difficult is it to present this truth to those you know?

_____

_____

_____

_____

_____

**2.** In what ways do the three words of John 14:6—*way, truth, life*—reverse the effects of the fall into sin suffered by Adam and Eve and the entire human race in Genesis 3?

_____

_____

_____

_____

_____

**3.** Suppose you told someone, "Jesus is the way." Suppose they said, "Oh yeah, the way to what?" How would you answer that question?

_____

_____

_____

_____

_____

**4.** If Jesus really is the only way to God, how do we explain our complacency? If we really believed John 14:6 in a way that deeply and emotionally moved us, how would our lives be different?

_____

_____

_____

_____

**5.** In this chapter, it was stated that "we have become such nice Christians. We never want to offend anyone." What is meant by that? Is it possible to be too nice of a Christian?

_____

_____

_____

_____

"*There is majesty in the name of God, there is personality in the name of Jehovah, there is power in the name of the Lord, there's unction in the name of Christ, there's affinity in the name of Emmanuel, there's intercession in the name Mediator, there's help in the name Advocate, but there is salvation in no other name than the name of Jesus.*"

~ Source Unknown

# CHAPTER SIX

# Why Do Christians Have So Many Problems?

AMONG THE TONS OF BIOGRAPHIES I'VE READ over the years, few have been more gripping and challenging than the story of Howard Rutledge, who spent seven years as a prisoner of war in North Vietnam. His book, *In the Presence of Mine Enemies*, tells how he survived the better part of a decade of suffering and torture after his plane was shot down during the Vietnam War. He was captured, stripped, and incarcerated. As he described his treatment, I shuddered at the cruelties he suffered. I'll spare you the graphic scenes of torture, but in one section of the book, he talks about the miserable state of his life as a POW: "When the door slammed and the key turned in that rusty, iron lock, a feeling of utter loneliness swept over me. I lay down on the cold cement slab in my six-by-six prison. The smell of human excrement burned my nostrils. A rat, as large as a small cat, scampered across the slab beside me. The walls and floors and ceilings were caked with filth. Bars covered a tiny window high above the door. I was cold and hungry. My body ached from swollen joints and sprained muscles. . . .

"It's hard to describe what solitary confinement can do to unnerve and defeat a man. You quickly tire of standing up or of sitting down; sleeping or being awake. There are no books, no paper, no pencils or magazines. The only colors that you see are drab gray and dirty brown. Months or years may go by when you don't see the sunrise or the moon, green grass or flowers. You are locked in, alone and silent in your filthy little cell, breathing stale, rotten air and trying somehow to keep your sanity."[1]

As I read Rutledge's story, I asked myself how human beings could treat other human beings with such sadistic evil, how they could inflict so much physical and psychological pain on one another. And, of course, I had to ask myself why God would allow it. That's one of the great mysteries of life—why does God allow suffering? As I'll share at the end of this chapter, Rutledge found a handful of incredible answers during his years of imprisonment, and the answers all pointed to the Lord Jesus. Still, the question remains: "Why do Christians have so many problems?"

Perhaps you're overwhelmed right now with multiple distresses. As you're reading this book you may feel tired because you didn't sleep well last night; your rest was hindered by bad dreams or anxious thoughts. Or maybe you're diving into this chapter truly needing a word from the Lord regarding what's happening in your life just now. Jesus told us problems would come our way. At the end of

His Upper Room Discourse on the eve of His crucifixion, our Lord's final words were, "In the world you will have tribulation; but be of good cheer, I have overcome the world" (John 16:33).

I wish I could sit down personally with everyone reading this book and listen to your burdens and pray with you. I'm not able to do that, of course; but I can seek to encourage you by sharing one of the Bible's great stories of tribulation and triumph, the story of the Old Testament hero Joseph.

Much of Genesis is devoted to Joseph's story, and God gave us his example as an encouragement amid the problems of life. Here was a young man, loved by his father and clad in colorful robes, who was betrayed by his brothers when he was seventeen years old. They wanted to kill him, but at the last moment they changed their minds and sold him into slavery. Joseph was dragged away to Egypt to be auctioned off at the slave market. A royal official named Potiphar purchased him, and at first Joseph's situation seemed to improve. He won the respect of his master and became steward of Potiphar's household. But when Potiphar's wife tried to seduce him and lure him into bed, Joseph resisted and fled, leaving his cloak in her hands. She accused him of rape, and Joseph, though innocent, was thrown into an Egyptian dungeon where he languished throughout the entire decade of his twenties.

Occasionally today we'll read a newspaper account of someone convicted of a crime—perhaps a heinous sexual assault—and sent to prison for many years until new DNA evidence proves the prisoner was innocent all the time. It's horrible to think of the possibility of that happening to any of us, but that's what happened to Joseph.

There's not a soul on earth who would want to be in an Egyptian prison today, but imagine the conditions nearly 3,000 years ago. That's where Joseph found himself. Through no fault of his own, his life descended into a series of nightmares that lasted year after year and went from bad to worse. Why would God allow something like that to happen to him? Why does He allow suffering to come into our lives? Why has He put you in a difficult place today?

Problems are not pretty; they are not fun. In pointing out the possible blessings that may come from burdens, I don't want to minimize them. I've been through some very dark valleys in my life, and there were times I didn't want anyone telling me that my burdens were blessings in disguise. Yet we must be biblical in facing our problems, and the Bible takes a more hopeful attitude than our emotions may feel.

John Maxwell made the following commentary on the question of problems. Problems are:

Predictors—They will mold our future.

Reminders—We are not self-sufficient. We need God and others to help us.

Opportunities—They pull us out of our rut and cause us to think creatively.

Blessings—They open up doors that we usually do not go through.

Lessons—Each new challenge will be our teacher.

Everywhere—No place or person is excluded from them.

Messages—They warn us about potential disaster.

Solvable—No problem is without a solution. [2]

As we study the biblical example of Joseph, I pray that you'll be encouraged by his story. Joseph's life from seventeen to thirty was a series of horror stories, and near the end of this period he suffered a final crippling blow of disappointment. According to Genesis 40, two other men were tossed into prison one day with Joseph—Pharaoh's butler and baker. Both men had somehow angered their boss, who consigned them to the dungeon. One morning Joseph noticed that both men seemed to be in a state of deepened distress, so he asked why their faces were sad. Both had suffered very disturbing dreams during the night. The men felt their dreams had significance, but they didn't know how to interpret them. Assuring them that God could explain their dreams, Joseph asked the men to share them with him.

The butler had dreamed of a grapevine with three prominent branches which had grown, blossomed, and produced grapes. The butler had pressed the grapes into wine for Pharaoh's cup and given it to the king. Joseph immediately knew the meaning of the dream and told the man that after three days he would be restored to his position. Joseph then added, "Remember me when it is well with you, and please show kindness to me; make mention of me to Pharaoh, and get me out of his house. For indeed I was stolen away from the land of the Hebrews; and also I have done nothing here that they should put me into the dungeon" (verses 14-15).

Since the butler had received good news, the baker hopefully described his dream. He had seen three white baskets on his head, filled with all kinds of baked goods for Pharaoh. But a flock of birds came and ate the bread and pastries. Alas, this time the meaning wasn't promising. Joseph told the man plainly, "This is the interpretation of it: the three baskets are three days. Within three days Pharaoh will lift off your head from you and hang you on a tree; and the birds will eat your flesh from you" (Genesis 40:18-19).

Pharaoh's birthday occurred three days later and he threw a party for himself. He celebrated by restoring the butler and hanging the baker, just as Joseph predicted. Joseph undoubtedly had high hopes for his soon release. The butler was back in Pharaoh's presence and would surely intervene for him. But hours became days, and days became weeks, and weeks months. Hope gradually died away like a car battery when the lights are left on. We can't imagine the discouragement Joseph must have felt. As Proverbs 13:12 says, "Hope deferred makes the heart sick."

Have you felt anything like that? Are you discouraged just now, waiting for good news that hasn't come? Perhaps, like Joseph, your problems have been prolonged and chronic and crippling to your spirit.

Well, let's turn the page and see Joseph's situation from the fuller perspective of Scripture. None of this happened by accident; nothing here was random; and God had not forgotten or forsaken His young man. Over and over we read that the Lord was with Joseph (Genesis 39:2, 3, 21, 23). It was all turning to good in the end, albeit slowly. God had His reasons, purposes, and plans, which were not readily apparent at the time. And it seems to me that this story is a reminder to all of us that there are advantages in our difficulties and providence in our problems.

This doesn't trivialize our problems, but it does "truth-alize" them. It allows us to begin looking at them from a different perspective. The Bible is like a mirror (James 1:23). As we see ourselves reflected in Joseph's experiences, we can realize God has a purpose for each one of us. Difficulties crowd into the lives of all God's children; but in the midst of everything, God can teach, prepare, and use us, even amid the strain. I'll give you five suggestions as to why Christians have so many problems.

## Problems Provide Greater Opportunities

First, problems provide greater opportunities. As we read these chapters in Genesis and look back at Joseph's life from the perspective of history, we're struck at how God converted the problems into potentials. Missionary and author Isobel Kuhn wrote an account of her life, titled *In the Arena*, based on the concept that difficulties are God's way of providing an arena for our witness. "God taught me through the years to view my own trials as platforms in today's Arena," she wrote. "I thought this concept was original with me, but one day my husband found that Hudson Taylor had formed the same opinion many years ago. He said: 'Difficulties afford a platform upon which He can show Himself.'"[3]

As God's children, we need to learn how to look for platforms in our problems. Sometimes our "prisons" are "pulpits." There's an entire section of the New Testament called the "Prison Epistles" because Paul wrote them while incarcerated in Rome. The apostle John wrote the book of Revelation, which has brought us such blessing, while exiled on the island of Patmos. It was in prison that John Bunyan composed his great allegory we call *The Pilgrim's Progress*.

For most of us, the prison experience is not literal. Our limitations may be related to health or finance or a thousand other things. The key is looking around in any given set of circumstances to see if God is using them to open a door for us. Charles Colson was one of Richard Nixon's attorneys who later went to prison for his role in the Watergate scandal. He came to Christ and later established a great ministry to those behind bars. I remember hearing Chuck speak at a dinner where he closed his message with words to this effect: "My lowest days as a Christian (and there were low ones, seven months' worth of them in prison, to be exact) have been far more fulfilling and rewarding than all the days of glory in the White House."

I'd rather be a Christian with problems than a non-Christian without problems, for even in our distress, God is with us, redeeming our difficulties and using them as an arena for His glory and grace. William Secker, a seventeenth-century clergyman, observed the following about Joseph's trials: "If Joseph had not been Egypt's prisoner, he had never been Egypt's governor. The iron chains about his feet ushered in the golden chains about his neck."[4]

## Problems Promote Spiritual Maturity

The story of Joseph also teaches that problems promote spiritual growth and maturity. I can't think of another biblical character who experienced worse mistreatment than Joseph, apart from the Lord Jesus Himself. As you rewind the story of his life, it's not hard to realize he probably had it easy as a child, for he was Jacob's favorite son. While his brothers were working, Joseph enjoyed being the center of attention. I'll not go so far as to say he was pampered, but his status as the favored son certainly raised the ire of his brothers. To fulfill the role God intended for him, Joseph needed grit, backbone, and dogged resolution; and those muscles only develop in the gymnasiums of life.

Sometimes the Lord has to toughen us up. Before Joseph could become Prime Minister of Egypt, he needed fortitude and faith in God's sovereignty. Psalm 105:17-18 says, "He [God] sent a man before them—Joseph—who was sold as a slave. They hurt his feet with fetters, he was laid in irons." There's a marginal reading in my Bible that translates the last phrase as: "His soul came into iron." I read an old English translation that said, "Iron entered into his soul."

When Joseph came out of prison, he was an iron-souled man. He was a man of great wisdom, courage, and determination. When he ascended the heights of the Egyptian government, he carried a nation that was foreign to him through a terrible famine without even one sign of revolt from the people. He was prepared for the hardship of famine because he had experienced the hardship of prison.

God needs "iron-souled saints" today, and the only way iron gets into our souls is through suffering. When we hurt and endure problems something changes in our hearts as we become more spiritually mature. That's the plain teaching of Romans 5:3-5: "We also glory in tribulations, knowing that tribulation produces perseverance; and perseverance, character; and character, hope. Now hope does not disappoint, because the love of God has been poured out in our hearts by the Holy Spirit who was given to us."

This teaching is echoed in many places in Scripture. Hebrews 12:11 puts it like this: "Now no chastening seems to be joyful for the present, but painful; nevertheless, afterward it yields the peaceable fruit of righteousness to those who have been trained by it."

James 1:2-3 says, "My brethren, count it all joy when you fall into various trials, knowing that the testing of your faith produces patience. But let patience have its perfect work, that you may be perfect and complete, lacking nothing."

Peter told his readers, "Though now for a little while, if need be, you have been grieved by various trials, that the genuineness of your faith, being much more precious than gold that perishes, though it is tested by fire, may be found to praise, honor, and glory at the revelation of Jesus Christ" (1 Peter 1:6-7). Through affliction, "the Lord separates the sin He hates from the soul that He loves."[5]

It's odd to think about, but sometimes our attempts to help others out of difficulty may actually abort the process God intends for their growth. That's tough for me to write, because I'm a rescuer. I don't know about you, but I have four children and twelve grandchildren; and I'll do anything I can to help them out of difficulty. But just think of this—if Reuben had made good on his intentions to get Joseph out of the pit and return him to his father, Joseph would have missed out on the entire ministry God had in store for him. If Potiphar had rescued Joseph from the tortures of prison, Joseph would never have achieved greatness. The problems he faced were providential routes God used to guide him from where he was to where he would fulfill his purpose in life.

We should do all we can to help others, of course, but always prayerfully, in wisdom, and with a view toward furthering the work of God in their lives. It's through hardship that God fires our soul with steel to face the challenges that are ahead. Problems promote our maturity.

## Problems Prove Integrity

Problems also prove our integrity. Our character, if genuine, is never altered by circumstances. Joseph was a man of great character, and every problem provided another opportunity to deepen and demonstrate the sterling nature of his integrity. Nothing so exemplifies our character as how we face difficulties.

Character is often confused for reputation, but there's a vast difference. Reputation is what others suppose we are; character is what we really are. Reputation is what those around you think of you; character is what God knows you to be. Reputation is what's chiseled on your tombstone; character is what the angels say about you before the throne of God. Character never changes with the circumstances; it's simply deepened by the difficulties.

Sometimes I hear people blame their circumstances for their poor choices. "The situation made me this way," they say. "I was forced by events to take this step. My background is to blame." That's not entirely true. Our backgrounds or circumstances may try to pull us downward, but we have the ability to choose our own convictions. Our situations reveal the way we are. When we face the difficulties of life, it's a wonderful opportunity for God to use us to demonstrate the reality and the integrity of our character before others.

On a hillside in rural Pennsylvania, a number of elaborate tombstones sprout from the ground, bearing long inscriptions of curious verse. But a nearby gravestone bears a simpler inscription. It identifies a woman named Margaret Workizer, who passed away February 4, 1805, at the age of 55, and adds these lines with their mild rebuke:

> *Verses on tombstones are but idly spent,*
> *The living character is the monument.*[6]

Mrs. Workizer made her point. The flashy and flamboyant are worth little. It's integrity, character, and humble faithfulness that leave a lasting mark. God likes characters with character. The steady is better than the showy, and godliness beats grandstanding.[7] We never have a better chance of displaying that before God and the world as when beset with difficulty. If you're facing some problems now, make sure to prevail through them with solid and Christlike integrity.

## Problems Produce a Sense of Dependency

Here's another thing about problems. They produce a healthy sense of dependency as it relates to our faith in God. They drive us to the Lord and teach us to lean on Him. As I said earlier, the Lord was with Joseph at every step; and by the end of the process, Joseph's faith was solid enough for him to tell the brothers who had kidnapped and sold him into slavery, "But as for you, you meant evil against me; but God meant it for good, in order to bring it about as it is this day, to save many people alive. Now therefore, do not be afraid; I will provide for you and your little ones" (Genesis 50:20-21).

> *"Pain and trials are almost constant companions, but never enemies. They drive me into His sovereign arms. There He takes my disappointments and works everything together for good."*[8]
>
> ~ KAY ARTHUR

William Griffith Thomas, the Anglican cleric and scholar, wrote about this in his devotional commentary: "The secret of Joseph's power was the consciousness of the presence of God. God had not forgotten him, though it might have seemed to him that it was the case. The very incident that was apparently the most injurious was the link used by God to bring about Joseph's exaltation. To the man who is sure that he is in the pathway of God's will, there will come the consciousness of the divine presence and blessing, which will be an unspeakable comfort as he rests in the Lord and waits patiently for Him. Evil may have its temporary victories, but they are only temporary. Good, and right, and truth, must prevail, and it is for the servants of God to wait quietly, to go forward humbly, to live faithfully, and to trust boldly, until God shall justify them by His divine interposition, and glorify His grace in their lives."[9]

Do you know what Joseph discovered while in prison? He found out how much God loved him. In my own experience, it's during the crises of life that I have made the most spiritual advancement. I'm sure that's true for you as well. I can't count the number of times people have told me when they've gone through family problems, or marital problems, or financial problems, or physical problems: "Pastor, I knew God loved me, and I've always felt close to Him; but I have never in my days felt His love as I've experienced it in the pressure cooker of what I've just gone through."

Author Tim Keller wrote, "One of the main ways we move from abstract knowledge about God to a personal encounter with Him as a living reality is through the furnace of affliction . . . Believers understand many doctrinal truths in the mind, but those truths seldom make the journey down into the heart except through disappointment, failure, and loss. As a man who seemed about to lose both his career and his family once said to me, 'I always knew, in principle, that "Jesus is all I need" to get through. But you don't really know Jesus is all you need until Jesus is all you have.'"[10]

## Problems Prepare Our Hearts for Ministry

Problems also prepare our hearts for ministry. You might say that prison was God's seminary to train Joseph in the skills later needed to lead the nation of Egypt. As a teenager, Joseph had dreamed of the sun, moon, and stars bowing down to him (Genesis 37:9). But by the time he was about thirty, he understood that leadership was serving others. I'm impressed with his concern for the butler and baker in Genesis 40. Here was a man who had languished for many years in a dungeon, yet was observant of the needs of others. He noticed two new prisoners who were downcast of countenance and he asked the reason. When they told him, he interpreted their dreams. Joseph could have wrapped himself in the cloak of self-pity, but here he was seeking to serve others. As Paul said in 2 Corinthians 1:4, we are able to comfort others with the same comfort we ourselves have received from the Lord.

When we're thrown into the difficulties of life, it makes us especially sensitive to others who have similar difficulties or parallel problems. Those who have found the grace of God in the middle of some catastrophic event are often called upon to share this grace with others. Many ministries have been launched in this way. Suffering brings about a heart for ministry. How are we to ever put our arms around a brother who is facing grave disappointment or bereavement if we have never experienced it ourselves? My ability to understand and comfort those battling cancer was totally different after I faced this terrible disease myself.

According to the book of Hebrews, even Jesus, the Son of God incarnate, experienced suffering in order to identify with our suffering.[11]

One pastor explained it this way: "Brokenness precedes usefulness. It just does. Who reaches out to parents who have lost children to drunken driving accidents? Other parents who have lost children to drunken-driving accidents. When we go through something painful and when God breaks us, it makes us both more useful to others and more willing to be used. We are able to empathize and sympathize and lend insight and help and perspective to other people. Take a poll of people you know in ministry, and I guarantee you'll find that some kind of painful experience informed their sense of call. People minister out of their own suffering, not despite it."[12]

Here, then, is a great lesson to encourage our hearts. Sometimes we have problems because God wants to get us ready to help somebody else. Because of what you're facing now, you'll be better equipped to reach others in the future. From his prison experience, Joseph became a servant of the world, standing day after day, administering grain to the hungry people. Where did he learn that? God broke his heart in prison and made a servant out of him. Pastor and author Robert Morgan observed: "Joseph went from the pasture to the pit, from the pit to the prison, and from the prison to the palace—and every step along the way God was with him, causing all things to work together for good under the omnipotent hand and omniscient mind of His sovereignty."[13]

Problems, then, though painful are profitable. They have advantages. They provide us with greater opportunities, promote our spiritual maturity, prove our integrity, produce a healthy sense of dependency on our Lord, and prepare our hearts for future ministry. That's exactly what happened to Howard Rutledge, the Vietnam War POW I introduced at the start of this chapter.

As soon as he was seized, Rutledge began to turn his thoughts to the Lord. After being shot out of the sky, captured, paraded around and abused, he was thrown into the first of many prison cells, and he later wrote these words about that moment: "I was alone for the first time since my capture. Reviewing the events of the day made me aware of one thing: It was a miracle that I was alive. I had not thought about God much since dropping out of Sunday school in my late teens, but lying on the floor, I could not help but think of Him then. . . . I had no idea what my fate would be, but the Lord had made Himself abundantly clear. He was there with me in the presence of my enemies."[14]

Terrible sessions followed with his tormentors, but through it all Rutledge learned to lean into God. "In the past," he wrote, "I usually worked or played hard on Sundays and had no time for church . . . I was too busy, too preoccupied, to spend one or two short hours a week thinking about the really important things.

"Now the sights and sounds and smells of death were all around me. My hunger for spiritual food soon outdid my hunger for a steak. Now I wanted to know about that part of me that will never die. Now I wanted to talk about God and Christ and the church. But in Heartbreak Hotel, the nickname of the most infamous POW prison in North Vietnam, solitary confinement, there was no pastor, no Sunday school teacher, no Bible, no hymnbook, no community of believers to guide and sustain me. I had completely neglected the spiritual dimensions of my life. It took prison to show me how empty life is without God, and so I had to go back in my memory to those Sunday School days in the Nogales Avenue Baptist Church, Tulsa, Oklahoma. If I couldn't have a Bible and hymnbook, I would try to rebuild them in my mind. I worked desperately to recall snatches of Scripture, sermons, the gospel choruses from childhood, and the hymns we sang in church."[15]

He also wrote about realizing how he had let down his family spiritually. "I had dropped out of church almost immediately after marriage and left my family to develop their spiritual life on their own. . . . I decided in Vietnam that if I were ever free again, I would try to listen, try to understand, and try to show spiritual leadership in my home and with my family."[16]

"I never stopped doing my daily routines," Rutledge said. "Some part of each day was filled with Scripture recall. We worked together to find more. Every man found some fragment of a Bible verse floating in his memory and contributed to the pile. Daily I would pray for my family and renew my resolve to make my commitment to Christ and join my family's church upon return to freedom. In prison I firmly believed there was a God who loved me and was working in my life. I cannot explain with reason or proof why my faith was central to my survival. But it was. Other men went in unbelieving and came out the same. I didn't; and for me, my faith in Christ made all the difference." [17]

Most of us want the crown, but not the Cross; Easter, but not Good Friday; the gain, but not the pain. But that's not the way it works, and that doesn't seem to represent the ways of God. In our lives individually, and in our families, and in our churches, God can take our problems and make us better—if only we cooperate with Him.

I'm so sorry if you're overwhelmed today, but don't give up. Visualize Joseph there with you and remember how God helped him. Think of Jesus beside you, and lean on Him. Exchange your problems for His peace, and let Him infuse your soul with His strength and His steel.

---

# QUESTIONS TO DISCUSS

**1.** This chapter opens and closes with the story of Navy pilot Howard Rutledge, whose years as a POW presented him with indescribable problems. Most of us haven't been POWs, but have you ever had a time in your life when your problems overwhelmed you?

_____

_____

_____

_____

_____

**2.** Joseph spent many years in slavery and in prison, but perhaps the cruelest blow was when the butler forgot him in Genesis 40. Why was that so hard? Can you recall anything in your experience that might parallel the disappointment Joseph felt?

_____

_____

_____

_____

_____

**3.** Joseph discovered that problems lead to opportunities. Can you think of other Bible characters who made the same discovery? Can you remember a problem in your life that later led to an opportunity you didn't anticipate?

_____

_____

_____

_____

_____


**4.** In this chapter, we read, "Sometimes our attempts to help others out of difficulty may actually abort the process God intends for their growth." How do we know when to "deliver" someone and when not to help them?

_____

_____

_____

_____

_____

**5.** What does the phrase "the sovereignty of God" mean to you? Why is this the ultimate answer to the way we look at life's difficulties?

_____

_____

_____

_____

_____

> *"Now I see that those things which so perplexed and tried me led to my greatest blessings. I could not then see the hand of the Lord in His dealings with me, but I see it plainly now. In that painful dispensation, in that sickness, in that trouble of mind, in that agony of soul, that distressed path, how plainly do I see now that the Lord's hand was leading me! And will it not be so for the future?"*[18]
>
> ~ James D. DeMarest, nineteenth-century Dutch Reformed pastor

# CHAPTER SEVEN

# Why Don't My Prayers Get Answered?

LIVING TO THE RICH AGE OF 94, Fanny Crosby is known as the Queen of Gospel Song Writers. She penned more than 8,000 hymns, each coming from her feisty but faithful heart. I never tire of reading about this blind genius, Fanny Crosby, who was also known for her independent streak, her dramatic speaking, her soul winning, and her tireless work in rescue missions. She died a hundred years ago, on February 12, 1915, but many of us still cherish her songs, like "Blessed Assurance," "To God Be the Glory," "All the Way My Savior Leads Me," "Redeemed," and "He Hideth My Soul."

Miss Crosby was blinded in infancy by a quack doctor who mistreated her inflamed eyes, and her poor mother and grandmother prayed earnestly for help and healing for her. They prayerfully took Fanny from one doctor to another, seeking a way to help the child regain her vision.

Their prayers were unanswered, but Fanny later admitted that her blindness was a providential gift. It led her to memorize vast amounts of Scripture, out of which streamed her incredible river of hymns. She later said of the errant doctor, "If I could meet him now, I would say, 'thank you, thank you' over and over again."[1]

Not long ago, the renowned organist Donald Hustad discovered a previously unpublished stash of Fanny's poems and hymns, and one of them was entirely devoted to praising God for the blessings of unanswered prayer. The title was "For What His Love Denies," and the manuscript was dated January 6, 1899. The first verse says:

> *God does not give me all I ask,*
> *nor answer as I pray;*
> *But, O, my cup is brimming o'er*
> *with blessings day by day.*
> *How oft the joy I thought withheld*
> *delights my longing eyes,*
> *And so I thank Him from my heart*
> *for what His love denies.*[2]

I'm often asked the question, "Why does God deny my requests? Why are my prayers unanswered?" Truth be told, I've sometimes asked that question myself. On various occasions in my life, I've been perplexed about God's apparent unresponsiveness to some of my specific prayer needs. But Fanny Crosby is right; God knows what He is doing and sometimes His denials and delays are benedictions. We are blessed by what He grants, and we are blessed by what He denies.

I'm also comforted by noticing how many biblical heroes grappled with the same issue. The Old Testament prophet Habakkuk asked, "O Lord, how long shall I cry, and You will not hear?" (Habakkuk 1:2) Jeremiah was equally troubled, saying, "Even when I cry and shout, He shuts out my prayer" (Lamentations 3:8). The patriarch Job said, "Oh, that the Almighty would answer me" (Job 31:35). David wrote, "O my God, I cry in the daytime, but You do not hear" (Psalm 22:2).

When we turn from the Old Testament to the Gospels, we find a similar pattern—an interesting assortment of requests Jesus denied. During His earthly ministry, our Lord didn't always say "Yes" to His petitioners. It's interesting how often He said "No."

Do you recall when the two ambitious brothers, James and John, aided by their mother, asked if they could sit to our Lord's left and right in the kingdom? They didn't know the implications of what they were asking, and the Lord didn't grant their request (Matthew 20:20-23). On another occasion, an unnamed man asked Him, "Teacher, tell my brother to divide the inheritance with me." Jesus replied, "Who made Me a judge or an arbitrator over you?" and He proceeded to warn the crowd against covetousness (Luke 12:13-15).

When Martha asked Jesus to tell her sister Mary to help with food preparation, Jesus wouldn't do it. "One thing is needed," He replied, "and Mary has chosen that good part, which will not be taken away from her" (Luke 10:38-42).

When a group of Pharisees and teachers asked Jesus for a sign, He turned them all down too, telling them bluntly, "An evil and adulterous generation seeks after a sign, and no sign will be given to it except the sign of the prophet Jonah" (Matthew 12:39). Later in the same chapter, our Lord's mother and brothers came, asking to see Him. Jesus again demurred (Matthew 12:48-50).

One of the most interesting "Nos" of Christ was to a man from whom He had cast out a legion of demons. The newly delivered fellow asked if he could follow Christ and travel with Him among the broader group of disciples. But Jesus had other plans for the man and told him "No." "Return to your own house," He said, "and tell what great things God has done for you" (Luke 8:39).

As we study these examples, a lesson emerges. Our Lord always knows what is best for us. He knows the future, the tomorrows we'll face, the strengths and weaknesses we possess, and the perfect nature of His preplanned will for us. Sometimes our momentary desires or earnest appeals aren't truly in our own best interests, and the Lord graciously says "No" or "Not yet."

And yet there are other occasions when we ourselves are the reason our prayers aren't answered. That's where I'd like to focus the remainder of this chapter. Sometimes our prayer requests aren't granted because there is something amiss in the one making the request, which would be us. I've gone through the Bible studying this subject, and I've found a number of specific Bible verses that help us answer the question at the beginning of this chapter: Why don't my prayers get answered? Sometimes it's because God knows better than we do what's for our good; but sometimes it's because there's something hindering our prayers on our end of the line.

Dr. J. Oswald Sanders wrote, "When a prudent businessman discovers that his business is running at a loss, he takes stock, draws up a balance sheet, discovers why he has made no profit, and takes remedial steps. Shall we be less prudent in our spiritual accounting? Have we ever sat down and honestly faced this question? Do we just accept the failure of some of our prayers fatalistically? Do we piously say, 'Perhaps it was not God's will after all?' Or do we ask honest questions."[3]

Well, let's be prudent stewards in the matter of prayer and honestly ask ourselves if there is something in our attitudes or habits that may prevent God from answering as freely as He would like. There are several places in His Word where God simply says that under certain circumstances He will not answer our prayers.

## Our Prayers Are Not Answered Because of Unoffered Prayers

The most obvious reason for unanswered prayer is that we haven't offered our prayers to begin with. In his wonderful little book *Master Secrets of Prayer*, Cameron V. Thompson wrote, "Surely heaven is overcrowded with answers to prayer for which no one has ever asked."[4] Several years ago I preached a sermon on this subject at Shadow Mountain Community Church. Our drama team presented a sketch before the message. The scene was the vestibule of heaven, and the props included a number of file cabinets stretching around the walls. A new resident of heaven entered the vestibule and asked about the cabinets. He was told there was a drawer with his name on it. When he inquired as to the contents, he learned it was full of things that God had wanted to give to him but had not because he had never asked for them.

In Cameron Thompson's book on prayer, he goes on to observe how we can read through hundreds of years of history in the Bible without a single petition being offered in prayer. For example, the first nine chapters of 1 Chronicles give us long and extended genealogies covering vast spans of time, one generation coming after another. But in the middle of the lineage, the list of names was interrupted to point out a man who took the time to offer a specific prayer: "And Jabez called on the God of Israel saying, 'Oh, that You would bless me indeed, and enlarge my territory, that Your hand would be with me, and that You would keep me from evil, that I may not cause pain!' So God granted him what he requested" (1 Chronicles 4:10).

So many of us needlessly live at a level far beneath that which God wants for us. He has a storehouse full of rich provisions, just waiting to be distributed to all those who will simply ask Him to open His hand. So often it is true that we have not because we ask not.

Why don't we bring our requests to God? Sometimes we simply don't take time for prayer. We're too busy to pray, or so we think. Recently the U.S. Department of Labor published the American Time Use Survey, showing how Americans in all fifty states spent every minute of their days in 2013, the most recent year with available records.

On average, social interactions took 43 minutes per day for most Americans. Employed citizens worked an average of 7.6 hours per day. Watching television accounted for 2.8 hours each day, and the average person spent 8.74 hours sleeping and 40 minutes a day on showering, putting on makeup, and so forth.

How much time does the average American invest in prayer each day? Monday through Friday, the tally averaged 5 minutes a day. On Saturday, the average jumped to 7 minutes, and on Sundays, 32 minutes.[5]

I hope you spend more than five minutes a day in prayer; but I'm afraid that in general terms most Christians spend far more time watching television (and even putting on makeup) than praying. In other words, we've not only forgotten how to sing the old hymn "Sweet Hour of Prayer," but we've also forgotten how to practice it.

Don't get me wrong. I'm not saying we have to be down on our knees for sixty minutes each day; we all have different routines and different schedules. But it's vital to build prayer into our routines and schedules and to spend time speaking to the Lord about the things we need. I'd be interested to know your prayer routine. Daniel had one that involved three private prayer sessions a day (Daniel 6:10), during which he prayed for specific needs (see Daniel 9:3-19).

It's helpful to be specific. Yes, there's a time for generalized praying, but if we want specific answers to prayer it's good to beseech the Lord for specific things. Burleigh Law, a missionary pilot in the Congo, was once trapped in a deadly sky by a storm that seemed to come from nowhere. There in the cockpit of his little missionary plane, he lost his bearings as thunderclouds surrounded him on every side. Here and there openings appeared in the clouds, and he kept turning his plane toward those openings, following little patches of blue like a needle through fabric. Finally he saw a little landing strip beneath him, and he landed with a sigh of relief. Suddenly a vehicle came racing up to his plane. A nurse ran to him, saying, "I don't know where you came from, but I know you are an answer to our prayers."

A missionary couple had been isolated on this remote mission station. The roads were impassable and the bridges were out. The wife had become seriously ill with a high fever. Early that morning the Christians in the village had gathered for earnest prayer for help. They had specifically asked God to somehow send help and intervene in the crisis. In response, God arranged the storm clouds in the sky to direct Burleigh Law's little plane to that very spot of earth.[6]

*"The greatest tragedy of life is not unanswered prayer, but unoffered prayer."[7]*

~ F. B. MEYER

If you're in trouble, pray, and pray specifically. If you're not in trouble, pray anyway. Pray when you feel like it and pray when you don't. Pray generally and pray particularly. Pray as unhurriedly as you can, and don't be afraid to pray about details and minutiae. God delights to deliver us in His own way and time through the power of our prayers.

## Our Prayers Are Not Answered Because of Unconfessed Sin

Another hindrance to answered prayer is unconfessed sin. Psalm 66:18 puts this plainly: "If I regard iniquity in my heart, the Lord will not hear." Please note that the verse doesn't say, "If I sin, the Lord will not hear me." We all sin, and our hearts are imperfect every day. Confession of sin is a regular part of a healthy prayer life.

But if we know there is definite sin in our lives without confessing it, it clogs up the prayer lines and hinders the answers. Those who "regard" iniquity hold particular sins in their hearts and make alibis for them. If you regard sin in your heart, you excuse it, tolerate it, neglect it, and cover it up. Regarding sin in our hearts, then, is not primarily the *fact* of sin but the *love* of sin. That's what blocks our prayer lives. The prayer God wants to hear from us is prescribed in 1 John 1:9: "If we confess our sins, He is faithful and just to forgive us our sins and to cleanse us from all unrighteousness."

John Bunyan, the author of *The Pilgrim's Progress*, added, "Prayer will make a man cease from sin, or sin will entice a man to cease from prayer."

This aspect of prayer is taught throughout Scripture; it's not limited to Psalm 66:18.

- "The Lord is far from the wicked, but He hears the prayer of the righteous."— PROVERBS 15:29

- "One who turns away his ear from hearing the law, even his prayer is an abomination."
  —PROVERBS 28:9

- "When you spread out your hands, I will hide My eyes from you; even though you make many prayers, I will not hear. Your hands are full of blood."—ISAIAH 1:15

- "Behold, the Lord's hand is not shortened, that it cannot save; nor His ear heavy, that it cannot hear. But your iniquities have separated you from your God; and your sins have hidden His face from you, so that He will not hear."
  —ISAIAH 59:1-2

- "Now some of the elders of Israel came to me and sat before me. And the Word of the Lord came to me, saying, 'Son of man, these men have set up their idols in their hearts, and put before them that which causes them to stumble into iniquity. Should I let Myself be inquired of at all by them?'"—EZEKIEL 14:1-3

- "For the eyes of the Lord are on the righteous, and His ears are open to their prayers; but the face of the Lord is against those who do evil."
  —1 PETER 3:12

When cyclist Lance Armstrong admitted to doping and lying, *USA Today* ran an article suggesting what the famous athlete had to do to get back into good graces with the public. The columnist said: "He just has to repent—or appear to," in four stages: Confession ("I did it"); Contrition ("I'm sorry I did it"); Conversion ("I will not do it again"); and Atonement ("I will do this because I did that").[8] Among today's failed celebrities, there's likely to be little true confession or repentance. They're more interested in damage control and media manipulation. But I found it interesting that the newspaper's advice had a biblical ring to it. God wove the elements of confession, contrition, conversion, and atonement into the process of restoration. And to restore our prayer lives to their maximum, it's important to learn the process of dealing with sin and walking with God. The Bible says, "If we walk in the light as He is in the light, we have fellowship with one another, and the blood of Jesus Christ His Son cleanses us from all sin" (1 John 1:7, where in its immediate context, "one another" refers to God and us). Learn to pray as Jesus taught us: "Forgive us our debts" (Matthew 6:12).

More than a hundred years ago, a college student in Wales named Evan Roberts felt a passion for revival. Returning to his village of Loughor, he preached to seventeen people, and his sermon had four points: (1) Confess any known sin to God and put away any wrong done to others; (2) put away any doubtful habit; (3) obey the Holy Spirit promptly; and (4) confess faith in Christ openly. By week's end, sixty people had been converted. Within three months 100,000 converts were added to the churches in Wales. The revival spread around the globe, and the years between 1904 and 1911 are remembered as the last years in which our world has experienced a truly global revival.[9]

## Our Prayers Are Not Answered Because of Unbelieving Minds

Here's another barricade to answered prayer—unbelief. The ever-practical epistle of James tells us to ask God for wisdom. "But," it warns, "ask in faith, with no doubting, for he who doubts is like a wave of the sea driven and tossed by the wind. For let not that man suppose that he will receive anything from the Lord; he is a double-minded man, unstable in all his ways" (James 1:6-8).

Jesus said in Mark 11:23-24, "For assuredly, I say to you, whoever says to this mountain, 'Be removed and be cast into the sea,' and does not doubt in his heart, but believes that those things he says will be done, he will have whatever he says. Therefore I say to you, whatever things you ask when you pray, believe that you receive them, and you will have them."

The Bible tells us it's impossible to please God without trusting Him, for those who come to God must believe that He exists and that He rewards those who diligently seek Him (see Hebrews 11:6).

Sometimes this is difficult to practice because we have to trust God to answer us in the best possible way. Some preachers declare a "name-it-and-claim-it" message to try to convince us we can have whatever we want if only we have enough faith. But the Bible says, "Now this is the confidence that we have in Him, that if we ask anything *according to His will*, He hears us. And if we know that He hears us, whatever we ask, we know that we have the petitions that we have asked of Him" (1 John 5:14-15, emphasis mine).

This passage in 1 John stresses the element of faith ("this is the confidence . . . if we know . . . we know"). But it also emphasizes the importance of praying "according to His will." The Bible tells us to pray, "Your will be done" (Matthew 6:10). James suggested we add these words to our requests: "If the Lord wills . . ." (James 4:15).

So there is a balance; we must pray in faith, but we must also pray according to God's will or in a way that reflects our surrender to God's will in any given situation. Let's say, for example, you want a brand new Lexus IS 250 C convertible. If you have enough faith, can you ask God for that car assured you will get it? Maybe you want it for good reasons, to transport people to church or to travel around on a preaching circuit. Perhaps it simply reflects your tastes or lifestyle. Will the "prayer of faith" bring that automobile to your garage?

The real prayer of faith is saying: "Lord, I'd love to have a brand new Lexus IS 250 C convertible, and if it's Your will, I know You can provide one at no cost or lead me to purchase one. Nothing is too hard for You. But if it's not Your will, I'm willing for You to substitute. The bottom line is that You know I need a car, so I'm going to tell you my desires and my needs and trust You for what's best. I'm not going to worry about it anymore."

Who knows? God's will for you might very well include a Lexus in your driveway; but how wonderful to know that, in any case, God is concerned about the specifics of our lives and has a perfect plan for every detail. We have a tremendous opportunity to exercise true faith when we find the balance between the prayer of faith and confidence in God's will. Our prayers are aided when we learn to pray with maturity: "Lord, I need this thing; I want this thing; I desire this outcome; I feel desperate for this solution and I ask You for it. Nevertheless, I also pray as Jesus did for Your will to be done in this matter. I trust You for what's best."

We then base our prayers on our wisest contemplations about a matter and trust God with the outcome. That is the true "prayer of faith." As someone said, don't pray, "Thy will be changed," but "Thy will be done."

## Our Prayers Are Not Answered Because of Unrighteous Motives

All that brings up another obstacle to answered prayer—inferior motivations. To me, this is quite difficult because we can't always trust our motivations. We often do good deeds for selfish reasons, and we sometimes ask God for greater things from lesser motivations. Going back to a passage I quoted previously, James wrote: "You do not have because you do not ask. You ask and do not receive, because you ask amiss, that you may spend it on your pleasures" (James 4:2-3). In the Bible translation called *The Voice*, this verse is translated: "When you ask, you still do not get what you want because your motives are all wrong—because you continually focus on self-indulgence."

I read about a small Christian group that was holding a convention. Outside the auditorium they displayed a motto, "JESUS ONLY." A strong wind blew the first three letters away and the sign read, "US ONLY." I'm afraid that many times we think we're doing something for Jesus when we are really doing it for us.

One of the greatest challenges to prayer is making our requests with well-motivated intentions, seeking the glory of God and the advancement of His name in all we want and do. I think you'll find Psalm 37:4 a great personal strategy, for it says, "Delight yourself also in the Lord, and He shall give you the desires of your heart." We can become introspective with our motivations—sometimes we should—but the best way to pray wisely is by delighting ourselves in the Lord. Don't simply look within; look above. Delight yourself in His Word. Delight in His presence. Delight in His promises. Delight in His work. Keep Jesus in the forefront of your mind; and when you pray, rejoice in Him.

This doesn't mean we cannot ask God to do something for those we love. We can still ask for our daily bread. But how wonderful to enjoy the Giver more than the gift, and to pray in the spirit of 1 Corinthians 10:31: "Therefore, whether you eat or drink, or whatever you do, do all to the glory of God."

One writer has explained it this way: "We must remember that God's ultimate concern is not with our team winning its ball game, but in Himself being glorified in our ball game. His ultimate concern is not that we all have perfect health, but that we lift up every ounce of our health to His honor. His ultimate concern is not that we have a high paying job . . . but that we praise Him for what He provides. His ultimate concern is that we are consumed with His glory in whatever state we are in. I believe that God delights in giving even the smallest of things to His children, but we must weigh the motives of our hearts against the substance of our requests. . . . The Bible plainly teaches that some people do not get what they ask for because they ask for the wrong reasons."[10]

## Our Prayers Are Not Answered Because of Unresolved Conflicts

Are there other reasons why our prayers aren't answered? Yes, according to the Bible our prayers may sometimes be unanswered because of unresolved conflict. Mark 11:25 says, "And whenever you stand praying, if you have anything against anyone, forgive him, that your Father in heaven may also forgive you your trespasses."

Jesus made the same point in His Sermon on the Mount: "Therefore if you bring your gift to the altar, and there remember that your brother has something against you, leave your gift there before the altar, and go your way. First be reconciled with your brother, and then come and offer your gift" (Matthew 5:23-24).

God made it clear in His Word that our acceptance with Him is based solely on the work He did for us at Calvary and in our belief in His Son as our only hope of salvation. But the Lord also told us in His Word that our fellowship with Him in prayer is conditioned upon our relationships with others. If I've offended my brother or sister, I need to go make things right—or at least try to—or my prayers may be hindered. If my brother has offended me, I must forgive him so bitterness won't be a barrier to my prayers.

Let me ask you as plainly as I can: Have you hurt someone but haven't tried to make it right? Or are you resentful at someone? People can hurt us, and some can hurt us in catastrophic ways. We can carry around bitterness for many years, but it's a self-destructive attitude and a prayer-hindering emotion. Ask God to give you a forgiving heart, and breathe out your prayers in an atmosphere of grace.

## Our Prayers Are Not Answered Because of Uncompassionate Hearts

As I searched the Scriptures looking for hurdles that hinder our prayers, I found another danger lurking in Proverbs 21:13: "Whoever shuts his ears to the cry of the poor will also cry himself and not be heard."

The apostle John also touches on this, saying, "Whoever has this world's goods, and sees his brother in need, and shuts up his heart from him, how does the love of God abide in him? My little children, let us not love in word or in tongue, but in deed and in truth. And by this we know that we are of the truth, and shall assure our hearts before Him. For if our heart condemns us, God is greater than our heart, and knows all things. Beloved, if our heart does not condemn us, we have confidence toward God. And whatever we ask we receive from Him, because we keep His commandments, and do those things that are pleasing in His sight" (1 John 3:17-22).

While we should be concerned about feeding the hungry of the world, I think these verses are specifically referring to having compassion on those we know who are in need. If someone needs our assistance and we refuse them—if we neglect them—we're violating our fellowship with God and it blocks His answers to our prayers.

## Our Prayers Are Not Answered Because of Unhealthy Marriages

I want to close this chapter with one other interesting verse on the subject, which tells us that our prayers may be unanswered if we aren't responsive to the person we've married. The Bible says, "Husbands, likewise, dwell with them [your wives] with understanding, giving honor to the wife, as to the weaker vessel, and as being heirs together of the grace of life, that your prayers may not be hindered" (1 Peter 3:7). The earlier verses in the chapter are addressed to wives, telling them how to respect and build up their husbands.

As a husband, if I don't have the right kind of relationship with my wife, Donna, it can hinder my ability to pray as powerfully as I should. I think Jesus touched on this same truth when He taught in Matthew 18:19-20: "Again I say to you that if two of you agree on earth concerning anything that they ask, it will be done for them by My Father in heaven. For where two or three are gathered together in My name, I am there in the midst of them." If we're doing our best to have fellowship with those closest to us—loving them and seeking to meet their needs—the harmony will carry over into our prayer lives. It's difficult to have a fight with your spouse and then go to a prayer meeting!

Think of it in terms of an electrical supply to your house or apartment. Our daily life depends on an uninterrupted supply of electricity. That's how our refrigerators stay cold and our heaters stay warm and our lights stay on. But sometimes a limb falls across the power line and service is interrupted. Sometimes a storm will blow down a transformer and the lights will go off. Nothing is quite right at home until the power is restored.

In talking with people who are concerned because God doesn't seem to be answering their prayers, Pastor Bill Hybels uses this outline he borrowed from a pastor friend of his:

- If the request is wrong, God says: *No*
- If the timing is wrong, God says: *Slow*
- If you are wrong, God says: *Grow*
- But if the request is right, the timing is right, and you are right, God says: *Go!*[11]

We need uninterrupted fellowship with the Lord; and if our prayer lives are hindered for even a short time, we need to restore service as soon as possible. In this chapter, I've gone through the Bible looking for verses about things that can interrupt the communication lines with heaven. For me, it's become a personal checklist, and I hope you'll treat it the same. We may not be getting the answers we need from God because of . . .

- Unoffered prayers
- Unconfessed sin
- Unbelieving minds
- Unrighteous motives
- Unresolved conflicts

- Uncompassionate hearts
- Unresponsive husbands and wives

Is there anything on that list troubling you? Psalm 86:5 says, "For You Lord are good, and ready to forgive, and abundant in mercy to all those who call upon You." We cannot afford to have our prayers hindered in days like these. We need constant access to the Throne of Grace, and we need to live in the Land of Answered Prayer.

As I wrote several years ago in my book, *Prayer: The Great Adventure*:

> From the beginning of the Bible to its conclusion, we see absolute evidence that God answers prayer. Things that we think are impossible, God does when people pray. Prayer has won victories over fire and earth and water. Prayer opened the Red Sea. Prayer brought water from the rock and bread from heaven. Prayer made the sun stand still. Prayer brought fire from the sky on Elijah's sacrifice. Prayer overthrew armies and healed the sick. Prayer raised the dead. Prayer has paved the way for the conversion of millions of people. When we pray, we align ourselves with the purposes of God and tap into the power of the Almighty. Because we pray, God works through us in ways that He wouldn't otherwise . . . God has determined that He will use the prayers of His people to accomplish His purposes on this earth. . . . If we want all the blessings God has available to give us, we, too, must pray.[12]

# QUESTIONS TO DISCUSS

**1.** Can you recall a time when you were disappointed with the way God answered or didn't answer a prayer that was important to you? Looking back, can you analyze why your request wasn't granted as you wished?

_____

_____

_____

_____

**2.** In this lesson we learned that some of our prayers are unanswered because they are unoffered. We think we're too busy to pray when, in fact, we should say, "I'm too busy *not* to pray." Describe your own prayer routines. How could you improve your daily prayer habits? How could you create a little more time each day for prayer?

_____

_____

_____

_____

**3.** Look up Psalm 139:23-24. How could these two verses help you in the area of unconfessed sin?

_____

_____

_____

**4.** What area of your life right now is most difficult for you to turn over to the Lord and to say, "Nevertheless not my will, but Yours, be done"?

_____

_____

_____

_____

_____

**5.** Think through your relationships. Is there someone toward whom you can be more compassionate? Someone who needs your forgiveness? If you are married, does the status of your marriage help or hinder your prayer life? How is the health of your human relationships reflected in your prayer life?

_____

_____

_____

_____

_____

> _"Nothing can so quickly cancel the frictions of life as prayers. Praying hearts . . . are forgiving hearts. So if we find ourselves growing angry at someone, pray for him—anger cannot live in the atmosphere of prayer."_[13]
>
> ~ William T. McElroy

# CHAPTER EIGHT

# Is There a Sin God Cannot Forgive?

"When my father was a young man," recalls evangelist Billy Graham, "he attended a revival meeting in North Carolina and became convinced through the sermon . . . that he had committed the unpardonable sin. And he lived with this awful thought many years. He agonized over it, was frightened by it, and thought of himself as a doomed man who could never repent of his sin."[1]

The elder Graham eventually found peace of mind in his understanding of the extent of God's mercy. But many people like him through history have been plagued by the fear of having committed the unpardonable sin. William Cowper, author of the hymn "There is a Fountain Filled with Blood," almost went out of his mind fearing he had committed the unforgivable sin.[2] Before finding assurance of his salvation, John Bunyan, the author of *The Pilgrim's*

*Progress*, was tormented by the thought that he had committed the unpardonable sin. "I feared therefore that this wicked sin of mine might be that sin unpardonable," he wrote in his memoirs, "nor did I ever so know as now what it was to be weary of my life yet afraid to die."[3]

The great evangelist Charles G. Finney wrestled with similar fears before finding peace in the Lord Jesus Christ. "I concluded that . . . I have grieved the Holy Spirit, and perhaps committed the unpardonable sin," he wrote in his autobiography.[4]

A generation or two ago, many old time pastors and evangelists traveled around the country conducting revival meetings in which they usually preached at least one sermon on the unpardonable sin. I recall hearing variations of this message when I was a child. Usually the preacher would ask the question, "What is the unpardonable sin?" Then he would work through a litany of sins that were common to his audience: Lying, stealing, selfishness, adultery, and so forth. After each, he would say something to this effect: "Yes, lying is a terrible sin, but it is not the unpardonable sin. The Lord Jesus will forgive you of that if you will come to Him in repentance." Not until the end of his message would the evangelist try to answer the question posed at the beginning, saying that while God will forgive us of all other repented sins, the one sin for which there is no pardon is that of the soul's final rejection of Jesus Christ as Savior.

It's been a while since I've heard a sermon on the unpardonable sin. That subject has somehow faded from our conversations at church, but it hasn't entirely disappeared from our hearts. One of the questions I'm regularly asked is, "Pastor, can I commit a sin that God cannot forgive?" Sometimes the question is framed like this: "Dr. Jeremiah, I think I've done something that God will not forgive. I've confessed my sin, but I don't feel God has forgiven me, and I can't forgive myself. Is it possible I've committed the unpardonable sin?"

My heart goes out to those who ask such questions, for they are undoubtedly carrying an overwhelming sense of guilt for something they've done in the past. How thankful I am when I can share with them the truths we talked about in our chapter on "How Can I Find Forgiveness?"

Yet we still need to be reminded of the unpardonable sin, because this is a subject Jesus Himself brought up in the Gospels. It is a biblical topic, and faithfulness to God's Word requires that we look into this question and see what the Scripture says. If there is an unforgivable sin, we need to know what it is so we can avoid it.

Jesus addressed the topic in Mark 3:20-30, a passage that ends with these words: "Assuredly, I say to you, all sins will be forgiven the sons of men, and whatever blasphemies they may utter; but he who blasphemes against the Holy Spirit never has forgiveness, but is subject to eternal condemnation" (Mark 3:28-29).

According to Jesus, there is one thing a person can do for which there is no forgiveness either in this age or in the age to come. There truly is an unforgivable sin. He described it as blaspheming against the Holy Spirit. But we are left wondering what those words really mean. What is the sin of blasphemy against the Holy Spirit? What is the unforgivable transgression?

The only way to understand those words is by studying them within the context of the overall passage. Whenever we study Scripture, it's vital to interpret the verses we read within their setting so we don't take things out of context. The passage here in Mark 3 concerns one very important question: Who is Jesus Christ? Everything depends on correctly identifying the Stranger of Galilee. In Mark 3:20-30, there were three opinions.

## To His Family Jesus Was Demented

In Mark 3:20-21, it appears the Lord's own family had concluded He was demented. The passage says, "Then the multitude came together again, so that they could not so much as eat bread. But when His own people heard about this, they went out to lay hold of Him, for they said, 'He is out of His mind.'"

The pressure and intensity of Jesus' ministry escalated to such an extent that there was no time for Him even to eat. Have you ever been so frantic you've forgotten to eat? My days are generally busy, but I almost always take time to eat. Occasionally on a Saturday when I'm all by myself, I may get so caught up in what I'm doing that I'll look at the clock and realize I've not eaten. But not often. Yet in Mark 3, our Lord and His disciples were skipping their meals because of the pressure of the crowds. They were overwhelmed by the multitudes jostling and pressing them for healing and for food and for deliverance from demons.

When the Lord's family back in Nazareth heard these reports, they became concerned and decided to stage a kind of intervention. Mark 3:21 says "His own people" thought He was out of His mind. This is referring to His mother and brothers, for they're the ones who show up at the end of the chapter to intervene and snatch Him away (see verses 31-35).

I'm not sure of their motivation in taking Jesus back home. His mother was undoubtedly motivated by love for Him, but His brothers were perhaps more worried about avoiding family notoriety or trying to restore some income from the carpentry shop. According to John 7:5, His brothers did not yet believe in Him. They thought He was crazy.

The same thing is liable to happen to you and me. Sooner or later, someone is going to call us crazy for following Christ. Don't be surprised when someone calls you "one of those crazy Christians." Don't worry about it. That's what they said of Christ; and the same thing also happened to the apostle Paul. In Acts 26, Paul made his legal defense before the Roman procurator of Judea, Porcius Festus. He recounted his conversion and shared his testimony and purpose in life. He was interrupted when Festus cried out in a loud voice, "Paul, you are beside yourself! Much learning is driving you mad!"

Paul responded, "I am not mad, most noble Festus, but speak the words of truth and reason" (Acts 26:25).

Some people think evangelicals are crazy. They think we're deranged because we believe in Jesus and trust the Bible. This is odd to me, because we Christians are certainly not people who believe in things despite the evidence. We believe *because* of the evidence, and our faith is sensible, logical, and satisfying. Our critics also have faith-based presuppositions, although they seldom think about that; and their evidence is far weaker than ours. Nevertheless, it's easy to brand Christians as being crazy.

Country music star Brad Paisley has a song that touches on the irony of this. It's called "Those Crazy Christians." The first several verses talk about the qualities of the Christian life that seem strange to skeptics—how Christians jump on airplanes and head to Africa and Haiti to risk their lives in Jesus' name, how we eagerly forgive others for just about anything, how we're likely to spend a sunny afternoon by the bedside of a stranger in a cold hospital room. Our behavior seems strange to the world. Skeptics think we are crazy. But the song ends by saying:

> *They look to heaven their whole life,*
> *And I think what if they're wrong?*
> *But what if they're right?*
> *You know, it's funny, much as I'm baffled by it all,*
> *If I ever really needed help, well, you know who I'd call*
> *Is those crazy Christians!*[5]

Paisley is a church-attending man, but he told *Parade Magazine* he tried to look at Christians as a skeptic would. "I wrote it shortly after my cousin-in-law passed away in 2011," Paisley said. "He was young, and he fought against a debilitating disease. There weren't five minutes of intensive care that there weren't at least two church members at the hospital, around the clock, and I remember thinking, what makes people take shifts for someone they haven't known very long? Well, it's belief."⁶

I'm not going to worry if someone calls me crazy for being a Christ follower, and neither should you. We can just answer in the words of 2 Corinthians 5:13: "If we are beside ourselves, it is for God; or if we are of sound mind, it is for you."

A similar term we can embrace is "radical." Mike Barrett wrote:

After traveling from Portland to Delhi looking for radical faith, here's the conclusion that I came to that might surprise you. Radical, in its origins, really means to be rooted. The idea behind the word is to be so grounded, so deeply rooted in a lifestyle direction that you stand against the social and cultural currents that tear others away from your path. It's not so much forcing a change of course, but returning yourself and others to an originally intended path. By this definition, classic radicalism is found in the lives of many historical figures, people who stood up for human rights and religious reform. Today, anyone who adheres to the person and teaching of Christ in the midst of a runaway humanism and hedonism is, by definition, a radical. It's essentially building your house on a rock that doesn't get torn down in cultural storms. So becoming a true radical is to return yourself and others to a sacred path, and stand against modernity's eroding influences.[7]

## To His Foes Jesus Was Demonic

The first reaction, then, to Christ was from His family. They thought He was demented. As we continue the story in Mark 3, we come across a much darker opinion of Jesus. His foes claimed He was demonic. Verse 22 says, "And the scribes who came down from Jerusalem said, 'He has Beelzebub,' and, 'By the ruler of the demons He casts out demons.'"

News had previously reached the religious leaders in Jerusalem about the excitement of our Lord's ministry and the enormous crowds He was attracting. A delegation of scribes came from Jerusalem to Galilee to see for themselves, and they witnessed Jesus' acts of healing the sick and casting out demons (verses 10-11). They couldn't deny His miracles. They couldn't dispute the changed lives. They had to acknowledge something amazing was occurring. Since they didn't accept Jesus as being sent from God, they went to the other extreme and accused Him of operating under the power and authority of the devil. They said He was demonic.

Don't be surprised if sooner or later the world calls you an evil person for following Christ. Our culture doesn't appreciate our biblical values, so they may accuse us of being bigoted or hateful or intolerant or evil. We're living in days when evil is called good, and good is called evil. The world and the Church have opposite values.

As we read about our Lord's response to the scribes, there's no indication He was upset or defensive. In this passage, He gives a thoughtful and logical set of answers. He began with a question: "How can Satan cast out Satan?" That statement elicited no response, for there was none to give; it was rhetorical and self-evident. The Lord then proceeded with three lines of argumentation.

First, Jesus used an illustration from the secular world: "If a kingdom is divided against itself, that kingdom cannot stand." If a nation becomes embroiled in a civil war, for example, it will not be able to fend off its enemies. If a country turns on itself, it's vulnerable to its foes.

Next, Jesus used a social illustration, saying, in verse 25, "And if a house is divided against itself, that house cannot stand." When a family tears itself apart, the home is lost.

Jesus concluded His reasoning with a spiritual illustration in verse 26: "And if Satan has risen up against himself, and is divided, he cannot stand, but has an end." In other words, if Satan is fighting Satan, then Satan is finished. Jesus implied here that Satan's kingdom is unified, cohesive, and powerful. It wasn't going to meet its doom from internal division, for it is united in its hatred of God and its opposition to Christ.

We can paraphrase the Lord's argument in this way: "It is not logical for you to accuse Me of casting out demons by the power of Satan. Your argument makes no sense. The most common observations in the political realm, the social realm, and the spiritual realm readily disprove your claims."

But Jesus wasn't finished. He went on to say in verse 27, "No one can enter a strong man's house and plunder his goods, unless he first binds the strong man. And then he will plunder his house." In other words, if a thief wants to steal the goods of a strong man, he must first subdue the strong man. The Lord was thinking here of Satan. To Jesus, Satan was a strong man whose house or kingdom dominates the earth. Jesus came to spoil the strong man's house by liberating those who are enslaved. That's only possible if the liberator (Jesus) is stronger than the strong man (Satan), which He certainly is. Jesus came to enter the strong man's house, bind him, plunder his goods, and free his victims. He was not working in collusion or cooperation with Satan. They are on diametrically opposite sides.

We can draw enormous hope from this simple illustration. The world may appear to be in Satan's hands. Everywhere we turn we see souls enslaved to sin, to self-destructive addictions, and to godless philosophies. World leaders loom over the headlines with threatening boasts and evil intent. We face wars and rumors of war, and it's hard to read the headlines without wondering if history is writhing in its death throes. But the name of Jesus is supreme. The person of Christ is powerful enough to send the most malevolent demons fleeing. There is more power in a single syllable from the lips of our Lord than in all the vaulting boasts of Satan and his hosts.

The power that Christ exercises over Satan has implications for us. One of my favorite New Testament verses is 1 John 4:4: "You are of God, little children, and have overcome them, because He who is in you is greater than he who is in the world." When we're in league with Jesus Christ, we have nothing to fear from Satan or his demons. We know who Jesus is, and that leads to our next observation in Mark 3.

## To His Followers Jesus Was Divine

As we continue studying this passage, it becomes apparent that we must believe certain things to be a true follower of Christ. In some of the most perplexing words He ever spoke, Jesus said in verses 28-30: "'Assuredly, I say to you, all sins will be forgiven the sons of men, and whatever blasphemies they may utter; but he who blasphemes against the Holy Spirit never has forgiveness, but is subject to eternal condemnation,' because they said, 'He has an unclean spirit.'"

I realize this is a difficult passage, and this paragraph has been the source of great misunderstandings in Christendom. It has frequently been mistaught and misquoted and misinterpreted. But it's important to drill into this text and discover what Jesus intended.

To arrive at the correct interpretation, we have to begin with the last phrase, which explains why Jesus made this statement. He gave this teaching because His foes were accusing Him of having an unclean spirit. Our Lord was telling them, in essence, "There is a sin that you are on the verge of committing. You should be very careful, because you're about to do something for which there is no forgiveness."

What was it?

Like the aforementioned preachers of yesteryear, let me take a moment and tell you what the unpardonable sin is not. It is not cursing Jesus. It is not adultery or sexual perversion. It is not murder or genocide. Nor is it suicide. I've often had heartbroken people come to me with anguished questions about this: "Pastor, my son or daughter or brother or mother took his or her own life. Is this the unpardonable sin? Does suicide mean my loved one will not go to heaven?"

No, suicide is not the unpardonable sin. Nor is it homosexual behavior or abortion or drug addiction. All these and many other things are damaging. They are reprehensible in God's sight. These are some of the very things that Christ died on the cross to forgive. But He *did* die on the cross to forgive them. That's why none of these things can be classified as the unpardonable sin.

Kay Arthur commented: "I've never met people any more tormented than those who believe they've committed the unpardonable sin. And sometimes they don't even know what it is. But somehow Satan has sown this lie in their hearts, and they believe him instead of running for refuge into what they know about God's character. They focus on this one sin and take it out of the context of the whole counsel of the Word of God."[8]

The unpardonable sin isn't something that someone commits randomly. The scribes who came from Jerusalem didn't just do this on a whim. They didn't simply show up without any preparation and happen to see Jesus doing miracles and react by saying, "Oh, that seems satanic!" If you follow the references to these scribes throughout the book of Mark you'll see there is a progression to their unbelief. They were initially curious about Jesus and His ministry. Then they had questions. In time, they grew indifferent; but then their indifference metastasized into a malicious attitude that became so hateful and vengeful that it ultimately nailed Jesus Christ to the cross.

In our story in Mark 3, there's an interesting fact that's apparent in the Greek New Testament but not readily obvious in the English. According to verse 22, the scribes said, "He has Beelzebub." The verb form for "said" is in the imperfect tense. It can be translated as, "They kept on saying." It wasn't just a matter of a sudden thoughtless word or an instant reaction. Their words represented a hardened attitude and an embittered and impenitent heart.

In his commentary on Matthew, Alfred Plummer wrote: "There is such a thing as opposition to divine influence, so persistent and deliberate, because of constant preference of darkness to light, that repentance, and therefore forgiveness, becomes impossible. The efficacy of divine grace remains undiminished, but the sinner has brought himself to such a condition that its operation on himself is excluded. Grace, like bodily food, may be rejected until the power to receive it is lost. Christ warns the Pharisees that they are perilously near to this condition. Against the dictates of reason and justice, they had deliberately treated as diabolical a work of the most surprising mercy and goodness."[9]

When God convicts us of sin and presents us with the Gospel, it's dangerous to neglect it, especially if our procrastination becomes chronic. We resist and resist and resist. After a while, we can become so hard-hearted and sin-hardened that we grow calloused of soul. Our ears can't receive the truth. Our minds shake off the conviction of the Spirit. We become cynical of conscience. And although the grace of God is still available to us, we push away from it.

The sin Jesus warned the scribes against was not like the sin committed by the woman taken in adultery. It wasn't like the sinful patterns of the woman Jesus met by the well in Samaria in John 4. It wasn't going to be committed by Nicodemus, who showed up with questions in the night in John 3. It wasn't even like the sin of denying Christ, which Peter committed.

These scribes had become Jesus-resistant because of the time-lapsed attitudes of their own evil hearts. It's tragic, for these scribes had devoted their lives to copying the Word of God. Note the relationship between the words *scribe* and *scribble*. These men had copied and recopied the Old Testament. Every day they sat down at a desk with a primitive pen and ink, and they opened an ancient scroll and began copying where they left off the day before.

They had copied Isaiah 53, about the Suffering Servant. They had copied Psalm 22, about the death of the Messiah. They knew Micah 5 and the prophecy of our Lord's birth. Yet their hearts had become so hardened they couldn't receive His grace when it arrived in personified form.

In *The Jesus You Can't Ignore*, John MacArthur made this comment: "These Pharisees were guilty of unpardonable sin because they knowingly—not in ignorance or by accident—but *deliberately*—wrote Jesus' work off as the work of the devil. Moreover, their rejection of Christ was a full, final, settled renunciation of Christ and everything

He stood for. Contrast their sin with that of Peter, who later denied knowing Christ and punctuated his denials with swearing and curses. But Peter found forgiveness for his sin. If we think carefully about what is happening here and what Jesus actually said, the notion of unpardonable sin is not really so mysterious."[10]

We can become hardened to spiritual truth by living in the middle of it. We can go to church so much it no longer makes any difference. We can read the Bible until it becomes like a blank stare and the words no longer register with us. The scribes had come to the place where they were so familiar with religious things that when the Son of God showed up, they didn't know who He was and they accused Him of being from Satan.

By ascribing the miracles of Jesus to Satan, the religious leaders were denying the deity of Jesus Christ. They were saying He could not be God. Yet by His miracles He was showing Himself to be nothing and no one less than God. Only God Himself could do what He had done. His followers believed in His deity.

It's the Holy Spirit who witnesses to the deity of Christ in our world today. So when you refuse to accept the ministry of the Holy Spirit or you ascribe His ministry to Satan, you give up the final opportunity. You have to believe in Jesus as the Son of God. We have to accept the witness of the Holy Spirit and act upon the conviction He brings.

The late theologian Dr. B. H. Carroll said it this way: "If one blasphemes the Father, there still remains the Son and the Holy Spirit. If he blasphemes the Son, there is still the Holy Spirit. But if he blasphemes the Holy Spirit, there is none left. All of deity is gone. And so there is no recourse left for him. It is the end result of a gradual, habitual and growing enmity against God."[11]

The thought of an unforgivable sin has haunted sensitive people in every Christian century, and maybe it has haunted you. I want to be clear in saying that if you're bothered in your spirit that you may have committed a sin God will not forgive, the very fact that you have anxiety over that is evidence you've not committed the sin. If He is still working in your heart, it's not possible to have committed the unpardonable sin. The very fact that you're reading this book is a tremendous indication you've not committed the unforgivable sin described in the Gospel of Mark.

In its essence, the unforgivable sin is hardening your heart against God and repeatedly refusing to respond to His entreaties to your soul. By continuing to resist and reject the Lord, you build calluses on your soul until after a while the conviction of the Spirit of God no longer registers on your heart. Over a period of time you become hardened. You hear the Word of God and it makes no impact on you. If you die in that condition, there's no further forgiveness available. For those who reject Jesus Christ, there's no forgiveness anywhere else, anytime, either in this world or the next. He died for you, and if you reject that, there's no other sacrifice for sin.

So don't worry that you've committed the unpardonable sin. But if you don't know Jesus Christ as your personal Savior, be concerned that you might. If you've resisted Christ and refused Him as your Savior, and if you put down this book, walk across the street, and get hit by a truck or have a heart attack, you will have committed the unpardonable sin. You don't get a second chance after death. Whatever we do concerning Christ, we do in this life. Don't gamble that you will have time or that you can respond later. The Bible says, "Seek the Lord while He may be found, call upon Him while He is near" (Isaiah 55:6).

So here we are today after all these years, and there are still three opinions about who He is: His family thinks He's demented, His enemies think He's demonic, and His followers think He's divine. Could I suggest to you that all of us fall into the category of one of those opinions? As C. S. Lewis pointed out in his classic book *Mere Christianity*, there are really only three ways to explain Jesus Christ—either He is a lunatic, a liar, or Lord of all. We cannot simply say He was a great moral teacher. A man who said and did the things that Jesus said and did was either crazy, evil, or exactly who He claimed to be— Lord of lords and King of kings.

I'm here to tell you that Jesus is who He claims to be. He is the way, the truth, and the life. He is the only way to God. He is Son of God and Son of Man, our Savior, the Word made flesh, the Firstborn from the Dead. He is our Maker, Defender, Redeemer, and Friend. He is Christ the Lord, the Rock of Ages, the Sure Foundation, the Cornerstone. When He is your unforgettable Savior, you'll never have to worry about the unforgivable sin.

———o———

# QUESTIONS TO DISCUSS

**1.** Have you or anyone you've known ever been afraid of committing the unpardonable sin?

_____

_____

_____

_____

_____

**2.** Are you afraid of being called one of those "crazy" Christians? How likely is that to happen to you? Who would most likely ridicule you like this? How closely would your response mirror that of Jesus and the apostle Paul?

_____

_____

_____

_____

_____

**3.** Does Satan try to trouble you? How much should we fear him?

_____

_____

_____

_____

_____

**4.** What would you say to someone in anguish over a loved one who committed suicide and who feared that was the unpardonable sin?

_____

_____

_____

_____

_____

**5.** How would you explain the unpardonable sin to someone who asked you to describe it? How can we best avoid the anxiety some have felt over this mysterious and ominous sin?

_____

_____

_____

_____

_____

*"No single act is unforgivable. The unforgivable sin is a continuous, ongoing rejection of forgiveness. Those who refuse forgiveness through Christ will spend eternity separated from His love and grace. Conversely, those who sincerely desire forgiveness can be absolutely certain that God will never spurn them."*[12]

~ Hank Hanegraaff

# CHAPTER NINE

# What Is Faith?

"How do you like to go up in a swing," asked Robert Louis Stevenson in a childhood poem many of us can still quote from memory, "Up in the air so blue? Oh, I do think it the pleasantest thing ever a child can do."

But maybe not; it depends on who's pushing the swing. In her book on trusting God, Christian songwriter and author Sheila Walsh recalls a summer's day from her youth when she and her big sister, Frances, went to a local park. They ran to the swing set, and Frances pushed Sheila back and forth, higher and higher. Eventually Frances grew tired and sat down on the grass. A boy known as the neighborhood bully came up and began pushing. Sheila was helpless to stop him because she couldn't let go of the chains without falling. "I was terrified," she recalls. "He wasn't pushing it any higher than my sister had, but I didn't trust him. I cried and cried until my sister told him to stop."

Looking back on the incident, Sheila learned a lesson. "The matter, you see, came down to a five-letter word: trust. Trust made flying high in the air an exhilarating experience, and when trust was absent, the swing turned into a nightmare."[1]

*Faith* is a five-letter word too, and it's a biblical synonym for trust. But trust and faith aren't simply Christian affairs. Everyone on earth operates by faith every day and in everything we do. When you fill up your vehicle, you trust the gasoline station to have the right product in their tanks. If you ever encounter a filling station that pumps water into your gasoline tank, you'll lose faith in it and take your business elsewhere. When you drive through a green light, you trust the city fathers to make sure the other lane is red. We want to live in a society in which we can trust our government, our police officers, and our utility companies. Whether we are Christians or atheists, it matters to us whether we can trust our friends and our spouses and our employers. It makes a difference whether you trust the pilot flying the plane or the doctor removing your appendix.

Faith and trust are a part of our lives from the moment we're born. Everyone leads a faith-based life, and if someone ever ridicules you for being a "person of faith," well, when they point the finger at you there are three fingers pointing back at them. We all live our lives by faith. The question is, What is faith, and are the objects of our faith trustworthy?

Visit a college bulletin board or the wall of a factory's break room and you'll see a lot of slogan-centered philosophies about this.

- When your faith is stronger than your fears, you can make your dreams happen.

- Faith is taking the first step even when you cannot see the whole staircase.

- Faith is the bridge between where I am and where I am going.

- Faith is the bird that still sings when the night is dark.

There's no lack of motivational motto-makers or poetic positive thinkers. But I've got a better slogan for you. It's not as sentimental, but it's more scriptural: "Now faith is the substance of things hoped for, the evidence of things not seen. For by it the elders obtained a good testimony. By faith we understand that the worlds were framed by the word of God, so that the things which are seen were not made from things which are visible. . . . But without faith it is impossible to please Him, for he who comes to God must believe that He is, and that He is a rewarder of those who diligently seek Him" (Hebrews 11:1-3, 6).

That Scripture reference is from Hebrews 11, known as the Bible's "Faith Hall of Fame." The book of Hebrews was written to a group of people facing discouraging times, and in chapter 10 the writer called on them to persevere and to press on without giving up, exhorting them, "Do not cast away your confidence, which has great reward. For you have need of endurance" (Hebrews 10:35-36). Hebrews 10 offers some clues about the people to whom this book was originally written. They evidently had started out for Christ with enthusiasm and had braved a season of persecution, but now they were older, wearier, and daunted by the prospect of more trouble (see Hebrews 10:32-35). They were discouraged. Some were disheartened. Some had stopped attending church (verse 25). Some were in danger of reverting back to their old way of life. All of us know how easily we can relapse into former patterns. Sometimes we take a step forward and two steps backward. Sometimes we stagger under the pressures of the day. But Hebrews 10:36 says, "You need to persevere so that when you have done the will of God, you will receive what He has promised" (NIV).

The writer went on to say in verse 38 that perseverance requires walking by faith, and he quoted from the book of Habakkuk: "The just shall live by faith" (see Habakkuk 2:4). That paves the way for the next passage in Hebrews—chapter 11, which we call the "Faith Chapter" of the Bible. The writer of Hebrews wants to remind his readers of the heroes of the Old Testament who also faced great adversity but who trusted God nonetheless. From their examples we learn what it means to live by faith and to walk by faith.

Hebrews 11 is known by its recurring phrase, "By faith . . . ." When we read this passage we could easily think of the sermonic technique used by Dr. Martin Luther King, Jr.—the technique of the recurring phrase. He would take a phrase and let it build, time after time in his speeches, until he reached a crescendo. "I have a dream today," he said over and over at the Lincoln Memorial in 1963, each usage of that phrase more intense than the last. It takes a great orator to spin a message around a powerful recurring phrase like that, but that's what we have in Hebrews 11: "By faith . . . by faith . . . by faith . . . ." That word occurs 24 times in this one chapter. Other well-known chapters in the Bible are recognized for their particular emphasis as well:

- The Resurrection Chapter—1 CORINTHIANS 15

- The Christmas Chapter—LUKE 2

- The Shepherd Chapter—PSALM 23

- The Virtuous Woman Chapter—PROVERBS 31

- The Abiding in Christ Chapter—JOHN 15

- The Creation Chapter—GENESIS 1

- The Love Chapter—1 CORINTHIANS 13

As we study Hebrews 11, try to imagine you've never heard the word *faith* before. Let's try to read this chapter with fresh eyes. Evangelist Ron Dunn said, "Some words are like drapes that have faded from long exposure to the sun. Frequent use has drained the color from their meaning until they are no longer recognizable. Such words need, from time to time, to be reexamined to insure that their use is consistent with their meaning. And 'faith' is a word dangerously close to fading. As Paul Tillich suggested, the word 'faith' itself must be healed before it can be used to heal people."[2]

What, then, is faith?

## The Description of Faith

Verse 1 begins with this classic definition: "Now faith is the substance of things hoped for, the evidence of things not seen." This description of faith is accurate. It begins by telling us faith is the realization of things hoped for. The word *substance* means "assurance" or "realization." The writer is saying, "Now faith is the realization of things hoped for." We can substitute the word *confidence*. What is faith? It's the confidence or assurance that what we hope for—the promises and realities of God—are true and available.

John MacArthur explained it like this: "Faith transports God's promises into the present tense. In other words, real faith implicitly takes God at His Word. Faith is a supernatural confidence in—and therefore reliance on—the One who has made the promises. It is not an uncertain hope for something that may come to pass in a vague, indefinite hereafter. It is a trust that brings absolute here-and-now certainty to 'things hoped for.'"[3]

Faith says that what God has promised will happen, and it's so certain that it's almost as if it has already happened. Faith treats things that are hoped for as a reality. The future is made real for men and women of faith. Faith is not ambiguous; it is not unsure. It is a concrete conviction. It is the present-day confidence of a future reality. Faith is the solid, unshakeable confidence in God that is built upon the assurance that He is faithful to His promises.

People can sometimes take one look at us and tell if we're living with confidence or if we're falling apart. Faith is confidence in what we hope for. As Christians we have certain expectations from what our Bibles say. We expect all things to work together for those who love the Lord. We expect Him to do exceedingly abundantly above all we could ask or imagine. We expect Christ to come again at any moment, like a thief in the night. We expect a city with foundations, whose builder and maker is God. We expect to live forever, for God has promised us everlasting life. We expect the Lord to take care of us, to know our needs before we even ask. These are the things we hope for, and when we go through life with confidence in these things—that is faith. Someone with faith lives in the absolute confidence that those things are factual, they are accurate, they are reliable, they are unfailingly true.[4]

The verse goes on to say faith is "the evidence of things not seen." What do we not see right now? We don't see God; He's invisible to us. We don't see Jesus Christ; He's removed from us. We don't see the angels—as a general rule. We don't see the spiritual realm or the Golden City of New Jerusalem. We also don't presently see all the solutions to all our problems, nor everything as everything should be. We do not yet see these things, but we have total assurance these realities and resolutions are just as real as the chair in which you're sitting or the building in which you're living. This is the way the writer of Hebrews defines faith.[5]

John Phillips wrote, "Faith gives substance to the unseen realities. Faith is a kind of spiritual 'sixth sense' that enables the believer to take a firm hold upon the unseen world and bring it into the realm of experience. All our senses do this. The eye takes hold upon the light waves that pulsate through space and make real to a person the things he sees. The ear picks up the sound waves and translates them into hearing.

"But there is a whole spectrum of waves beyond the range of the senses. We cannot see them or hear them or taste them or smell them or feel them. But they are real, and with the aid of modern instruments, we can pick them up and translate them into phenomena that our senses can handle. Faith reaches out into the *spiritual* dimension and gives form and substance to heavenly spiritual realities in such a way that the soul can appreciate them and grasp them and live in the enjoyment of them."[6]

Many people believe faith is vague and unreal, like trying to believe that fairy stories are actually true. Nothing could be more mistaken. Faith is a reality, and it reaches out to facts that are solid—more real, more substantial, and more eternal than anything registered by our physical senses.

The apostle Peter touched on this when he wrote: "whom having not seen you love. Though now you do not see Him, yet believing, you rejoice with joy inexpressible and full of glory, receiving the end of your faith—the salvation of your souls" (1 Peter 1:8-9).

Faith is not lacking in reality. Faith is more real than your seeing and your hearing and your smelling and your tasting and your touching. Faith is far more real than any of the senses God has given you. Faith is not just the sixth sense; it's the supreme sense.

People of faith are prepared to live out their life believing God. Their lives reflect a commitment that's unbelievable to people who don't know Jesus. They're so sure of the promises and so sure of the blessings that they behave as if those promises have already been realized.

Many of us have read the story of Katie Davis, who at the age of eighteen became a teacher of kindergarten children in Uganda. While she was there God led her to adopt Ugandan children. Now she leads a great ministry and has written about her experiences in *Kisses from Katie*. She described how her life became a balancing act between running a nonprofit organization that required enormous amounts of

> *"Faith is deliberate confidence in the character of God whose ways you may not understand at the time."[7]*
>
> ~ OSWALD CHAMBERS

money and being a mother to her orphans. "Both aspects were testing and growing my faith in marvelous ways," she said, "as I learned to trust God to provide material needs as well as wisdom and courage to parent the precious lives with which He had entrusted me."[8]

Biblical faith is a growing confidence in the unseen reality of God and His involvement in our lives, even in times of stress. In fact, were it not for times of trouble, we wouldn't have as much reason to grow in our faith. When you read Hebrews 11, every single one of the twenty-seven or so people whose names are written there had one thing in common: By faith they surmounted unbelievable obstacles.

As we look at these men and women—Abel, Enoch, Noah, Abraham, Sarah, and the rest—we see that faith begins with perception. It's impossible to have saving faith unless your mind embraces the content of truth. You don't just get faith by putting your Bible under your pillow at night. You don't get faith in some emotional experience. Faith starts with truth, with opening God's Word. "Faith comes by hearing, and hearing by the word of God" (Romans 10:17).

Someone wrote, "When any new fact enters the human mind it must proceed to make itself at home; it must proceed to introduce itself to the previous denizens of the house. That process of introduction of new facts is called thinking. And, contrary to what seems to be quite generally supposed, thinking cannot be avoided by the Christian."[9]

God allows you to hear truth, and that truth comes into your mind, and that truth begins to interact with what you already know. We think. Faith involves the intellect. It involves thinking. The Word of God gets into the mind of a person and begins to intermingle with what's already there, and that thinking process is called perception.

But perception itself cannot be faith. Just knowing something isn't faith. You have to add the element of persuasion. What you are thinking has to penetrate into your emotions. You become emotionally attached to that truth. As you think about the truth it begins to play upon your heart. You begin to turn it over in your mind until it becomes part of your emotional makeup.

But perception and persuasion are not enough. When we truly exercise our faith, it requires performance. We have to act on our faith. We have to put it into action. It requires our whole being—mind, emotion, and will.

I read about three people who were trapped in a cave in which the water was rising. One of these men was a philosopher, another was a scientist, and the third was a peasant. None of them could swim. Fortunately emergency responders discovered their plight, and rescuers lowered a rope harness to save them. The philosopher said, "Well, this looks like a rope, but perhaps it's an illusion." He didn't attach himself to it, and he drowned. The scientist felt he should study the rope, and his calculations raised questions as to its strength. He delivered a lecture about the analysis of the rope's physical and chemical properties. But he didn't attach himself to it and he drowned. The simple man said, "Well, I don't know if it's a rope or a python tail, but it's my only chance, so I'm grabbing it and holding on for dear life." He alone was saved.[10]

Real faith grabs hold of the truth and hangs on. Real faith doesn't bypass the mind or the emotion, but neither does it bypass the will. Real faith says, "I believe it. I receive it. I base my actions on it."

## The Demonstration of Faith

Hebrews 11 goes on to say that the object of our faith—Almighty God—is the Creator of the universe, and that our faith begins when we recognize His handiwork in what He has made: "Now faith is the substance of things hoped for, the evidence of things not seen. For by it the elders obtained a good testimony. By faith we understand that the worlds were framed by the word of God, so that the things which are seen were not made of things which are visible."

In other words, faith sees the invisible; and faith realizes the visible world has come from the mind of the invisible God. What an incredible text! Our culture is at war over this very topic, and one of the most provocative questions in our public discourse is: "Where did we come from?"

The atheists and evolutionists claim it's not scientific to approach this question from a background of faith. Yet that is exactly what they are doing.

You and I know that faith in God gives us an understanding of the universe. God created the worlds by His word. The first sentence of the Bible says, "In the beginning God created the heavens and the earth" (Genesis 1:1). The psalmist said: "By the word of the Lord the heavens were made, and all the host of them by the breath of His mouth. . . . For He spoke, and it was done; He commanded, and it stood fast" (Psalm 33:6, 9).

What we see—the material universe—was not made by material things. An unseen power created what we see. The cosmos was made by God.

If you don't believe that—well, you still believe. You believe everything happened by accident or by random processes. Where did the substance and the processes come from to begin with? You have no explanation. All of the men I know who are atheistic evolutionists can reason all they want to until they get to the beginning of it all. But even when they discuss the Big Bang, they have no idea where the original elements came from. They have no way of knowing. They simply believe in materialism without any evidence or explanation. They say evolution is a scientific theory, but I suggest it's actually unscientific. It's a hypothesis more than a theory. It cannot be tested. It cannot be proven, and many of its tenets have been disproven. To me, it takes a lot more "faith" to be an evolutionist than it does to be a Christian. "The heavens declare the glory of God" (Psalm 19:1). And by faith we understand the worlds were framed by God, so that the things which are seen were not made of things which are visible.

## The Demands of Faith

That brings us full circle to the demands of faith, for verse 6 says plainly, "But without faith it is impossible to please Him, for he who comes to God must believe that He is, and that He is a rewarder of those who diligently seek Him." Faith is essential. The Lord demands it as part of a healthy relationship with Him. You cannot please God without faith. It's part of the DNA of a Christian.

> *"The beginning of faith is simply believing that God is."*[11]
> ~ JOHN MACARTHUR

It's important to God that we believe that He *is* and that we seriously seek Him. The Bible says that if we will seek God, He will be found. Isaiah 55:6 says, "Seek the Lord while He may be found, call upon Him while He is near." Jeremiah 29:13 says, "And you will seek Me and find Me, when you search for Me with all your heart." Amos wrote, "For thus says the Lord to the house of Israel: 'Seek Me and live'" (Amos 5:4). Jesus said, "But seek first the kingdom of God and His righteousness, and all these things shall be added to you" (Matthew 6:33).

If you tell me you're not sure you really believe in God, my question to you is, "Yes, but are you really searching for Him? Are you really seeking after Him? How much do you care? How serious is your quest? What have you read that has helped you understand who God is and what God does? How seriously have you investigated the truth about God in the Bible?" According to Hebrews 11, God will reward those who seek Him, and those who seek Him will be found by Him.

There are many stories about people in places where the Gospel has never been preached but who have followed the knowledge that was available to them only to find themselves in front of somebody who knew about Jesus and who told them how they could know God. I don't pretend to understand it all, but that's what the Word of God says. I believe that when people respond to the light God gives them, He will send more light. He honors those who seek Him.

He also blesses us as we find and trust Him. The remainder of Hebrews 11 is filled with the names of people who are my favorite characters in the Bible. They made the Hall of Fame. These are some of God's best people. There are twenty-seven of them by name, and many other unnamed ones. The writer of Hebrews 11 started with Genesis and, like a lot of preachers, spent so much time on the first part of his message that he had to abbreviate the last part. I love how he says in verse 32, "And what more shall I say? For the time would fail me to tell of . . ." and he has to summarize his remaining points. How often I feel that way in preaching! But as you read this roster of heroes, you sense that *faith* is what the Bible stories were designed to teach us.

Hebrews 11 begins with the Creation, talks about Abel, talks about Enoch, talks about Noah, and goes through the book of Genesis, showing us over and over that these were people who chose to exercise faith in adversity. The writer moved into Exodus, then touched on Joshua and Judges, and then he just gave up trying to list more examples. He was saying to his readers: Don't get discouraged and don't give up. God has given you a book—the Bible—filled with one story after another to teach you the importance of living and walking by faith.

And what a faith! Since, like the writer of Hebrews, I'm running out of room in this chapter, let me summarize chapter 11 like this:

- Faith brings the proper sacrifice.
- Faith enables one to walk with God.
- Faith builds an ark when it has never rained.
- Faith goes out not knowing where it's going.
- Faith dwells in tents in a foreign country.
- Faith looks for a city whose builder and maker is God.
- Faith receives strength to bear a child when the mother is past the age of childbearing.
- Faith offers up one's own son in obedience.
- Faith believes in the Resurrection.
- Faith promises not to leave Jacob's bones in Egypt.

- Faith refuses to be called the son of Pharaoh's daughter.

- Faith chooses to suffer affliction with the people of God.

- Faith esteems the reproach of Christ greater riches than the treasures of Egypt.

- Faith forsakes Egypt for the Promised Land.

- Faith passes through the Red Sea as on dry ground.

- Faith walks around Jericho till the walls fall down.

- Faith subdues kingdoms, works righteousness, obtains promises.

- Faith stops the mouths of lions and quenches the violence of fire.

- Faith escapes the edge of the sword and turns flight to the enemies of aliens.

- Faith receives the dead back to life and faith receives the promise.

- And faith comforts those who are not delivered from suffering and death on this earth.

So don't let anybody tell you, "Oh, faith is just a feeling." No, faith is something that happens. Faith acts. Faith empowers you. In my copy of the Bible, I went through Hebrews 11 and underlined all the verbs. It was astounding. When I read the following list of verbs to my congregation at Shadow Mountain Community Church, I could see their faces brighten with every successive term: Faith obtains, understands, offers, pleases, prepares, obeys, goes out, waits, receives, embraces, confesses, declares, seeks, desires, offers, concludes, blesses, worships, mentions, refuses, chooses, esteems, looks, forsakes, fears, endures, keeps, passes, encircles, works, obtains, stops, quenches, escapes, and becomes.

Faith pleases the heart of God. When you face difficulties, trust the Lord and press on as joyfully as you can. When the devil knocks the wind out of you, regain your spiritual breathing and let the Lord lift you up. When you're overwhelmed in the flood, regain your emotional bearings and look up. When confronting daunting challenges, cling to the cross of Christ and rest your hope on things eternal. God responded to the faith of the ancients, and He responds to ours.

Houston pastor John Bisagno described a time when his daughter Melodye Jan, age 5, came to him and asked for a doll house. John promptly nodded and promised to build her one, and then he went back to reading his book. Soon he glanced out the study window and saw her arms filled with dishes, toys, and dolls, making trip after trip until she had a great pile of playthings in the yard. He asked his wife what Melodye Jan was doing.

"Oh, you promised to build her a doll house, and she believes you. She's just getting ready for it."

"You could have thought I'd been hit by an atom bomb," John later said. "I threw aside that book, raced to the lumber yard for supplies, and quickly built that little girl a doll house. Now why did I respond? Because I wanted to? No. Because she deserved it? No. Her daddy had given his word and she believed it and acted upon it. When I saw her faith, nothing could keep me from carrying out my word."[12]

Don't misunderstand me when I say our faith isn't primarily in God's Word, but in His Person. Yes, we do trust the Bible. But the reason the Bible is trustworthy is because its Author is unfailing. The reason we rely on His promises is because He cannot lie. Our God is eternally unchanging, truthful, omniscient, and faithful, so His promises and precepts are the same. Scripture didn't breathe out God, but God breathed out the Scripture; and the reason we study the Bible is to learn more about Him.

> *"I believe the promises of God enough to venture an eternity on them."[13]*
> ~ ISAAC WATTS

Faith responds to the promise of the Father. And His most foundational promise is this: If we will place our faith in His Son alone for eternal life, He will save us from our sins and give us the gift of eternal life. We will spend eternity with Him in a place that is even now being prepared for those who will put their trust in Jesus Christ. That's the best place to begin the life of faith.

Luci Swindoll, a popular speaker and the sister of my friend Chuck Swindoll, wrote this about her mother: "In many ways, it was she who taught me to trust the Lord. She introduced my two brothers and me to Christ when we were children and even though she's been in glory for almost forty years, there's hardly a day that goes by I don't think of her. In some ways, she drove me crazy. By nature, Mother was moody, artistic, controlling . . . yet wonderful.

We rarely knew how she was going to be when she got up in the morning. Having a capricious temperament made her unpredictable, but God used that to help me lean on Him all the more, as well as become closer and closer to my father."

Luci went on to describe periods of stress with her mom, and she spoke of how her father's patience helped her cope with her mother's impetuousness. Both parents played a part in her spiritual development, and both in their own way helped her learn the lessons of faith. "I learned to trust God because He's the only One who can make things happen," she wrote. "It's not my mother or father in whom I've put my trust. It's not my siblings. It's not my friends or coworkers. It's not my peers. It is God.

"Sometimes, the hardest thing in the world is to trust God. It requires letting go of my preference and waiting for Him to lead. But that's how I'd like to live the rest of my days on earth . . . Who knows how many years I have left? Nobody. But I know the One in whom I have put my trust, and it is He who matters the most." [14]

You can do that too. You can trust Him with the years you have left, whether few or many. The roll call of the heroes of the faith isn't closed; new names are being added in the heavenly records every day. Jesus said, "Have faith in God" (Mark 11:22), and a songster of old worked this phrase into a hymn when he penned: "Have faith in God, He's on His throne; Have faith in God, He watches o'er His own. He cannot fail, He must prevail; Have faith in God, have faith in God." [15]

# QUESTIONS TO DISCUSS

**1.** If someone asked you for your definition of the word *faith*, how would you answer?

_____

_____

_____

_____

**2.** Look up the following passages and make a list of other biblical ways of defining faith: Proverbs 3:5-6; John 4:50; Luke 1:38; Luke 1:45; Acts 27:25; and Romans 4:21. Add Hebrews 11:1 and determine which of these definitions of faith is your favorite.

_____

_____

_____

_____

**3.** Is it hard for you to have faith in the invisible realm? Is such faith sensible or illogical?

_____

_____

_____

_____

**4.** Atheistic evolutionists actually exercise faith just as much as believers in a Creator do. Do you agree? Do you think it takes more "faith" to believe in evolution than in creation?

_____

_____

_____

_____

_____

**5.** Are you facing a situation requiring faith right now? What truth or application from this chapter is most helpful to you in meeting your current challenge?

_____

_____

_____

_____

_____

*"Faith always has been the mark of God's servants, from the beginning of the world . . . It is a firm persuasion and expectation, that God will perform all He has promised to us in Christ."*[16]

~ Matthew Henry

# CHAPTER TEN

# What Is the Greatest Commandment?

DORIAN "DOC" PASKOWITZ, who recently passed away at age 93, is remembered as one of the most important personalities in the history of surfing. He rode his first wave on the Texas coast at age 12, became a lifeguard at Mission Beach in San Diego in 1946, and later moved to Israel where he hit the beaches near the Gaza Strip and surfed every day. He was still riding the waves in his 90s. He told people who asked him about his top priority: "The greatest thing in life is health."[1]

What is the greatest thing in life? As we come to the end of our discussion of questions Christians are asking, we might as well close with the ultimate question of all—What is more important than anything else? What's scribbled at the top of your list of things of greatest value? What is our ultimate duty?

How would you answer those questions if they were posed in a questionnaire or interview? If someone in the coffee shop asked, "What's the greatest thing in the world for you?" what would be your spontaneous answer?

Entertainer Taylor Swift said, "I think it's the most important thing in life to dance to the beat of your own drum and to look like you're having more fun than the people who look cool, like they fit in."[2]

Motivational speaker Amanda Gore says that the most important thing in life is how you feel about yourself.[3] Actress Audrey Hepburn said, "The most important thing is to enjoy your life—to be happy—that's all that matters."[4]

Mitch Albom, author of *Tuesdays with Morrie* said, "The most important thing in life is to learn how to give out love, and to let it come in."[5]

Oprah Winfrey interviewed Paulo Coelho, the author of *The Alchemist*, a best seller that broke the world record for a book most translated and written by a living author. Oprah asked him to isolate the one quality necessary to be a truly spiritual person. He told her the most important quality was not necessarily belief in God. Rather it is this one thing—courage. "Courage is the first spiritual quality that you need to have," he said.[6]

At the opening of each Olympiad, the gathered athletes recite the Olympic Creed, which was adapted from a speech given at the 1908 Olympics by Episcopal Bishop Ethelbert Talbot. It says: "The most important thing in the Olympic Games is not to win but to take part, just as the most important thing in life is not the triumph but the struggle. The essential thing is not to have conquered but to have fought well."[7]

How would God answer the question about the most essential thing in life? We don't have to speculate about the answer, for an ancient scribe once asked that very question to Jesus of Nazareth, and we have our Lord's infallible response word for word. It's found in Mark 12, where Jesus was fielding a series of hostile questions posed by critics who were trying to trip Him up in His answers. It was the final week of His ministry, just a day or so before Calvary, and Jesus had entered the temple compound to debate His foes. They asked Him about taxes. They asked Him about the Resurrection. They expected Him to say something inflammatory or to incite the crowds, yet He spoke with such wisdom they couldn't fault Him for anything. Finally a certain man ventured a question. Mark 12:28 says, "Then one of the scribes came, and having heard them reasoning together, perceiving that He had answered them well, asked Him, 'Which is the first commandment of all?'"

## Searching for Answers

The tone of verse 28 seems to indicate that our Lord's questioner wasn't as hostile as the others. He was impressed at the way Jesus had handled the verbal hatchets thrown at Him. Perhaps this man was truly desirous of our Lord's insights. Perhaps he was searching for the answers to life's ultimate questions. I'm sympathetic to him, because later Jesus commended him for his attitude (see verse 34).

The questioner is described in verse 28 as "one of the scribes," indicating he was involved in a religious vocation, undoubtedly based in the temple precincts. A scribe copied the Scriptures for other people. He spent his days at a desk with a scroll, ink, pen, and blank parchment. He copied Old Testament books line by line; and as he did so, he obviously read the words, pondered them, and studied them. In those days, scribes were thought of as theologians. This man had probably copied every command in the Old Testament, and perhaps he wondered if they were all equally important or if one stood out above the rest.

From rabbinical sources we know the Jews divided the Law's commands into positive and negative ones. They counted 613 commandments in the Old Testament, 248 of which told us what to do. The other 365 told us what we shouldn't do. Some were "Thou shalts." Most were "Thou shalt nots."

And you thought there were only ten commandments!

The Ten Commandments are summary statements, but the remaining 600-plus give the specifics. These are the sub-commandments that describe various applications of the great principles of the Law. This scribe, then, was asking Jesus to walk into a room, as it were, to look at all 613 items on the table, and to instantly pick up the most important one.

Had you or I been answering his question, we might have suggested the first of the Ten Commandments, from Exodus 20:2-3: "I am the Lord your God, who brought you out of the land of Egypt, out of the house of bondage. You shall have no other gods before Me." It makes sense that the first command of the Ten Commandments would be the first commandment overall, the most important one.

But Jesus answered by going to another place in the Old Testament and quoting from the book of Deuteronomy: "The first of all the commandments is: 'Hear, O Israel, the Lord our God, the Lord is one. You shall love the Lord your God with all your heart, with all your soul, with all your mind, and with all your strength.' This is the first commandment."

That's Deuteronomy 6:4-5, written by Moses in his old age; and the opening word of this passage, "Hear," is the Hebrew term *Shema*. In Jewish usage, then, this text became known as the Shema: "Hear, O Israel . . . ."

By our Lord's day, the Shema had become the core of Old Testament teaching. In a way it was what John 3:16 is to us—the summary of all they believed and the first thing they memorized. Jewish children learned this as their first memory verse. Most Israelites repeated it twice a day, once in the morning and once at night. Still today this is the central prayer in the Jewish prayer book and is regularly recited in the synagogue and in Jewish gatherings.

According to the Shema in Deuteronomy 6 and the Savior in Mark 12, the most important thing we can do in life is to love the Lord our God.

Missionary Helen Roseveare wrote: "To love the Lord my God with all my soul will involve a spiritual cost. I'll have to give Him my heart, and let Him love through it whom and how He wills, even if this seems at times to break my heart.

"To love the Lord my God with all my heart will involve a volitional and emotional cost. I'll have to give Him my will, my rights to decide and choose, and all my relationships, for Him to guide and control, even when I cannot understand His reasoning.

"To love the Lord my God with all my mind will involve an intellectual cost. I must give Him my mind, my intelligence, my reasoning powers, and trust Him to work through them, even when He may appear to act in contradiction to common sense.

"To love the Lord my God with all my strength will involve a physical cost. I must give Him my body to indwell, and through which to speak, whether He chooses health or sickness, by strength or weakness, and trust Him utterly with the outcome."[8]

We were made to love God. When Adam and Eve lived in the Garden of Eden, God came and walked among them in unbroken fellowship. He loved them and they loved Him, and that was the normal state of things. That is the way it should be. The most terrible thing about the entrance of sin into the human bloodstream is that it stripped away the natural love we should have for God. Now we're prone to love the world instead, and all the things that are in the world (see 1 John 2:15).

The apostle Paul characterized the last days as being a time when people will be lovers of pleasure more than lovers of God (2 Timothy 3:4). The simplest definition of *idolatry* is "loving something or someone more than we love the Lord." That is fatal. The apostle Paul put it dramatically in 1 Corinthians 16:22 when he said, "If anyone does not love the Lord Jesus Christ, let him be accursed." The Aramaic expression is *anathema*. It means to be damned and cut off forever from the Lord.

We are made to love God, and our failure to love Him is the ultimate sin. The command to love Him is our greatest obligation and joy.

How, then, should we love God? Jesus went on to use some vital propositional phrases: "You shall love the Lord your God *with all your heart.*"

Some years ago, a man came to me with this question: "Dr. Jeremiah, my friend had a heart transplant. My friend wasn't a Christian, but the person who donated the heart was. Does that mean my friend is now a Christian?" I think I must have smiled at the question, but the answer is self-evident. When the Bible speaks of the heart, it's not talking about the fist-sized organ behind your sternum that serves as the center of your cardiovascular system. When we're to love the Lord with all our hearts, it has to do with our center of consciousness, with the source of our thoughts and personalities.

Almighty God doesn't want our *passive* love; He wants our *passionate* love. He told us to love Him with all our passion, from the very center of our being, from that which constitutes the real person within us.

Jesus didn't stop with our hearts; He also told us to love God *with all our soul.* What's the difference? How can we distinguish heart from soul? I believe the word *soul* conveys the volitional part of us, our determination to flip on the switch of our love. We make decisions with the soul. When we love the Lord with all our heart, it's like having our tanks filled with fuel; and when we love Him with all our soul, it's like turning on the ignition.

But that's not all. We're to also love the Lord *with all our mind*. Jesus added this to the Shema on the spot. This phrase wasn't originally in Deuteronomy 6:4-5. Since Jesus is God Himself, He can add editorial comments to His Word whenever He wants. With this one phrase from His lips, we went from having three ways of loving God to four. This simple addition is at the root of all Christian education. This is the truth that gave rise to Christian schools, universities, and all evangelical intellectual enterprises. This is why we have Christian philosophers, thinkers, writers, professors, scientists, and researchers. Our faith isn't compartmentalized in our emotional and volitional realms; it's at the root of our thinking. We love Him with all our mind.

Some people are so emotional in their religion they give the appearance of having shut their minds. That's not a balanced witness to the world, especially when some of these people show up on television with a presentation of the Gospel that plays on people's emotions but doesn't respect their minds. We need to love the Lord in an emotional way, of course, but we're also to love Him with a sharp intellect and with all our mind. James Emery White made this observation: "When summarizing human devotion to God as involving heart, soul, and strength, Jesus added, 'and mind' to the original wording of Deuteronomy, as if He wanted there to be no doubt that when contemplating the comprehensive nature of commitment and relationship with God, our intellect would not be overlooked."[9]

Gene Veith said it this way: "Everything the mind is capable of doing is to be devoted to loving God. It would seem then that if your mind can spin out complex mathematical calculations, you are to love God in mathematics. If your mind can plan a business, design a building, analyze a novel, understand a philosophical problem, or imagine a story, you are to love God in your planning, designing, analyzing, understanding, or imagining."[10]

God has given us minds, and those minds are His; He wants us to equip them and use them for His glory. Look up the word *mind* in the Bible and see how God emphasizes this. Here are some examples just from the book of Romans:

- "With the mind I myself serve the law of God."
  —ROMANS 7:25

- "To be spiritually minded is life and peace."
  —ROMANS 8:6

- "Be transformed by the renewing of your mind."
  —ROMANS 12:2

- "With one mind and one mouth glorify the God and Father of our Lord Jesus Christ."
  —ROMANS 15:6

The Bible says, "You will keep him in perfect peace, whose mind is stayed on You" (Isaiah 26:3). And, "Let this mind be in you which was also in Christ Jesus" (Philippians 2:5). We must love God with our thoughts. Whatever our callings and however God has wired us, we must use our minds for His honor.

God doesn't like laziness, and He doesn't like a lazy mind. I thank God for the men and women who encouraged me with their intellectual strength and giftedness—my mentors and professors and those from whom I'm still learning. I thank God for those who write books that make me think and who give talks that make me listen. I thank Him for the teachers He has raised up in my church and in every God-fearing congregation. I thank Him for the gifted minds of our young people, and I pray they'll learn to love the Lord with all their heart, soul, and mind. We can *thank* Him because we can *think* of Him.

We're to love the Lord our God with all our heart, all our soul, all our mind, and with *all our strength*. That's the last phrase in this quadratic command.

What does it mean to do something with all your strength? We almost never see that, even among athletes. Sometimes at a major sporting event like the Olympics we see athletes compete with all their strength, breaking records and putting every last ounce of energy into their events. To do something with all our strength implies intensity and sustained effort and ongoing concentration. That's the way we're to love God, and it's the most important thing we can ever do.

By gazing at the immense masterpiece of God's love—the Crucifixion—we can learn something about our two greatest duties in life—loving God and loving one another. Have you ever visited a museum and watched amateur artists setting up their easels before the canvases in order to imitate the masters? In the same way, when we set up the easel of the soul before Calvary, we learn to imitate the perfect love of the Master. There, on the old rugged cross, we learn something about the purposeful, selfless, unconditional, and sacrificial nature of God's love.

## Searching for Love

If you search out the word *love* in the Bible, you'll find a lot of verses about God's love for us and a host of verses about the love we should show others. But about fifty passages describe what it means for us to love God. One of the most convicting truths is that God notices and measures our love for Him. I know a lot of people who think that loving God is getting a warm, fuzzy feeling around their heart when they sing a hymn in church or when they pray or when they read the Bible. "I felt really close to God," they're apt to say. Well, that's good. Nothing's wrong with that. But the Bible specifies some other ways in which our love for God should be recognized.

We express our love for the Lord through obedience. Jesus said, "If you love me, keep my commands . . . . Whoever has my commands and keeps them is the one who loves me" (John 14:15, 21, NIV).

The apostle John wrote, "This is how we know that we love the children of God: by loving God and carrying out his commands. In fact, this is love for God: to keep his commands. And his commands are not burdensome" (1 John 5:2-3, NIV).

Our love for God can also be seen by our hatred of evil. Psalm 97:10 says, "You who love the Lord, hate evil!" If you're tolerating an evil pattern in your life, it betrays your love for God.

We show our love for God by conversing with Him in prayer. Psalm 116:1 says, "I love the Lord because He has heard my voice and my supplication."

Loving God also means we can hardly wait for His return. The apostle Paul, anticipating his own death and the Lord's return, wrote, "Finally, there is laid up for me the crown of righteousness, which the Lord, the righteous Judge, will give to me on that Day, and not to me only but also to all who have loved His appearing" (2 Timothy 4:8).

Over the past few years we've all seen videos on television of men and women in the Armed Forces who have returned home and surprised their loved ones. A little girl at school turns around, and there's her dad. A boy opens a big present under the Christmas tree, and out pops his dad. When we're away from those we love, we long for the time when we'll see them again. We long for a reunion. I believe the Lord placed the clouds in the sky and gave us beautiful sunrises and sunsets to remind us of our Lord's return. The last prayer of the Bible is, "Even so, come, Lord Jesus!" (Revelation 22:20) We can tell how much we love Jesus by determining how excited we are every day about His return and His Second Coming.

In a way we can't fully understand, God notices our actions and measures our love for Him. There's an interesting verse about this in Deuteronomy 13, where Moses told the Israelites, "If a prophet, or one who foretells by dreams, appears among you and announces to you a sign or wonder, and if the sign or wonder spoken of takes place, and the prophet says, 'Let us follow other gods' (gods you have not known) 'and let us worship them,' you must not listen to the words of that prophet or dreamer. The Lord your God is testing you to find out whether you love him with all your heart and with all your soul" (Deuteronomy 13:1-3, NIV).

God tests us to find out whether we really love Him as we should. There may come into your life a tremendously influential person. That person may charm and delight and amaze you. It might be someone of the opposite sex, or a buddy, or it might be a religious figure. But if that person tends to draw you away from the Lord, it's a test to see if you really love the Lord with all your heart, soul, mind, and strength.

In a similar way, at the end of John 21, the risen Christ appears to the apostle Peter and asks him a series of three questions, corresponding to the three times Peter denied Christ on the night of our Lord's arrest. "Simon, *son* of Jonah, do you love Me more than these?" (John 21:15)

The Lord asked that question over and over, until Peter was hurt. But Jesus was probing Peter's heart and helping him realize that he had to love the Lord with all his heart, soul, mind, and strength.

Apply this scene personally. If the risen Christ suddenly appeared to you in your living room or kitchen or in the front seat of your car, and if He were going to ask you one question, what do you think it would be? It might be about the most important thing in life, the most important question, about the most important and greatest thing we can ever do. He might look at you and say tenderly, "Do you really love Me?"

Carl J. Printz, Norway's Consul to Canada during World War II, lived a long life and left a deep legacy. When he was ninety-nine years old, Printz was interviewed on television. The journalist said, "Give us the rule you have followed during your long and useful life, the rule which has most influenced your life and molded your character." Printz replied, "I would mention one definite rule—one must be temperate in all things." But he paused and added, "Perhaps I should say temperate in all things except one—fulfilling the commandment to love God with all your heart, soul, and mind and your neighbor as yourself. These are the only things we can rightly do with excess."

## Searching for Meaning

In Mark 12, Jesus answered the scribe's question about the greatest command by telling him to love the Lord his God with all his heart, soul, mind, and strength. But Jesus didn't stop there. To live a truly meaningful life, we have to know the second greatest commandment. Mark 12:31 says, "And the second, like it, is this: 'You shall love your neighbor as yourself.' There is no other commandment greater than these."

Isn't it interesting that the scribe asked Jesus one question, and Jesus replied with two answers? Jesus told us to love God; then He went on to tell us to love our neighbor in the same way we'd like to be loved ourselves. This particular passage is repeated in other Gospels, and we call it the Golden Rule.

For example, Matthew 7:12 says, "Therefore, whatever you want men to do to you, do also to them, for this is the Law and the Prophets." Luke's Gospel renders it like this: "And just as you want men to do to you, you also do to them likewise" (Luke 6:31).

I love the Golden Rule, but it's important to remember that the Golden Rule cannot save us. It isn't comprehensive in its teaching. We can't get to heaven on the Golden Rule. If you stand before the Lord someday and He says, "Why should I let you into My heaven?" don't try saying, "Well, I kept the Golden Rule." The Golden Rule has no power to forgive your sin or justify you before God. It isn't the "end-all" of spirituality.

The Golden Rule is our Lord's explanation of how to implement His second commandment. If we want to understand what it means to love God, we have to love others; and if we really want to love others we have to treat them with kindness, fairness, gentleness, honesty, integrity, and servanthood—just as we ourselves want to be treated.

This theme is embedded into the Scriptures like paving stones. Philippians 2:4 says, "Let each of you look out not only for his own interests, but also for the interests of others." Romans 15:2 says, "Let each of us please his neighbor for his good, leading to edification." And 1 Corinthians 10:24 says, "Let no one seek his own, but each one the other's well-being."

If we love our neighbors as we love ourselves, we'll grieve over their lost job as we'd grieve if we lost ours. If one of their loved ones dies, we'll feel the pain. If we have problems with them, we'll seek to resolve them. Whenever they have a need, we'll try to fill it. The second commandment tells us to love others with action-based care.

In the days of the Bible, several Greek words could be translated as *love*. There was *eros*, which was a sensual love (our word *erotic* comes from it). There was *philia*, which was brotherly love (*Phila*delphia is the "city of brotherly love"). There was *ludus*, or playful love. But when Jesus came on the scene, a new word came into vogue. *Agape* was a term almost unknown before the presence of Jesus. It refers to a selfless love, the kind of love God has for us. This is the New Testament term for the way we should love one another.

God loves us with a selfless love because we have nothing in ourselves to offer Him. He loved us because it was in His heart to love us without any expectation that we could do anything to repay Him. That's the kind of love we're to express to our neighbors. Love isn't simply a warm, fuzzy feeling around your heart. It's an action word. When you love, you do something. When you love somebody, you do something for him or her.

Linda Didion was a cook in a Life Care Center in Massachusetts. She was industrious and always eager to brighten the plates and hearts of the residents. She knew they loved "turkey pot pie days," and she and her fellow cook made them painstakingly from scratch using an old recipe provided by one of the residents. One afternoon, Linda worked hard preparing the pies for the next day. She was almost finished when, about 7 or 8 p.m., she heard a loud crash. She turned to find that the tray containing about half the turkey pies had tumbled onto the floor.

As they looked at the mess, Linda's coworker lamented that they would have to substitute an alternate meal for the pies they lost. Linda drove home and went straight to bed for she had to get up early the next day. After tossing and turning half the night, she threw aside the covers, jumped out of bed, rushed to the overnight market, and bought all the items she needed. She finished baking the new pies at 3 a.m., and the next morning she came with enough pies for everyone.[11]

That's a better definition of love than you'll read in any book of poetry or hear on the radio. If you love your neighbors with *agape*, you don't stand around at the mailbox waiting to see if they sent you a thank-you note. You love them because it's the nature of God in you to treat them kindly without worrying about the response.

One of the ways to love your neighbor is to tell them about Jesus Christ. The Bible tells us to go into all the world and preach the Gospel to every creature. That's the Great Commission (see Matthew 28:18-20). This commandment Jesus has told us about in Mark 12 is called the Great Commandment. Here's a little formula I find helpful: A great commitment to the Great Commission and the Great Commandment will make great churches and great Christians.

Love does it all. Love fulfills all the rules, commands, and requirements of the Law. If we love God as we should, we'll automatically serve and honor Him. If we love others as we should, we'll habitually meet their needs. Galatians 5:14 says, "For all the law is fulfilled in one word, even in this: 'You shall love your neighbor as yourself.'" James

2:8 says loving our neighbor is the royal law according to the Scripture.

When you read the Ten Commandments in Exodus 20, you may notice that the first four have to do with our relationship with God. We're to have no other gods before Him; we're to avoid idolatry and using His name in vain; we're to honor His Sabbath Day.

The last six commands relate to the way we treat our neighbors. If we truly love our neighbors, we'll not lie to them, steal from them, kill them, or covet what they have. That's why the New Testament writers can say all of the Law hangs on these twin truths: Love God with all your heart; love your neighbor as yourself. These two commands summarize the Ten Commandments and they encompass all 613 commands in the Old Testament. In fact, every command in Scripture can fit into one of those two great overarching themes: loving God and loving others.

## Searching for the Kingdom

Now, as we come to the end of our story in Mark 13, we have an interesting postscript. The scribe who questioned Jesus about this apparently listened in rapt attention. He was intrigued by the Lord's words. He seemed to grasp the wisdom of them. It was like a lamp being switched on in his thinking, and it provided clarity for his years of Old Testament studies. He appreciated Jesus' words and told Him so despite the presence of the enemies hovering near.

"Well said, Teacher," he replied. "You have spoken the truth, for there is one God, and there is no other but He. And to love Him with all the heart, with all the understanding, with all the soul, and with all the strength, and to love one's neighbor as oneself, is more than all the whole burnt offerings and sacrifices" (Mark 12:32-33).

When Jesus heard those words and saw that he answered wisely, He said to him, "You are not far from the kingdom of God" (Mark 12:34).

This man was not yet in the kingdom, but he was closer to it than he had ever been. In fact, he was close to the kingdom because he was standing in front of the King Himself. I hope that scribe ended up going all the way. I think he probably did. I'm optimistic about this fellow. In the evangelization of Jerusalem after the Day of Pentecost, we're told, "The word of God spread, and the number of the disciples multiplied greatly in Jerusalem, and a great many of the priests were obedient to the faith" (Acts 6:7).

According to the records given to us in Acts, some of the vocational workers in the temple were saved. Some of those who had seen and heard Jesus in the temple courts trusted Him as their Messiah and their Master. Somehow I feel that our scribe from Mark 12 was among them.

But I don't know for sure. Here's what I do know: It's not good enough to be "not far from the kingdom." You want to be all the way in. A lot of people attend church every week. They may have some grasp of theology. Lots of people have a positive view of the person of Christ. Many try to live a good life; they like Christian music; they listen to Christian radio shows; they support worthy causes. They are not far from the kingdom. But only by trusting Christ as Savior can we actually enter into the kingdom of God.

How tragic to end your life with this epitaph: "He was not far from the kingdom."

Jesus said in Matthew 10:37-38: "Anyone who loves their father or mother more than Me is not worthy of Me; anyone who loves their son or daughter more than Me is not worthy of Me. Whoever does not take up their cross and follow Me is not worthy of Me."

That's a verse worth thinking about. I cannot tell you how much I love my children. Most parents can say the same. Our love for our kids is extraordinarily intense because they came from us, and we feel a bonding and a responsibility for them that endures as long as we live. When something goes wrong in their lives, it bothers us a thousand times more than if something goes wrong in our own lives. If they get sick, we wish we could get sick instead of them. If they have a crisis, we wish it would fall on us instead.

But Jesus said we should love Him more than we love our sons or daughters or parents or even our very own lives. How can He expect something like that? How could He say something like that? Because He knows that when He is in first place, all our other relationships will be healthier because of it. When we love Him first, we'll have His love flowing through us that will enrich our sons and daughters and fathers and mothers.

Loving Him is the first and greatest thing of all. We're to love the Lord our God with all our heart, soul, mind, and strength. The song of our heart is, "Oh, how I love Jesus!" The desire of our soul is, "More love, O Christ, to Thee." We love Him because He first loved us. He loves us with an everlasting love; and we are more than conquerors through Him who loves us.

What, then, is the greatest command? It's the simplest thing in the world—to love the Lord your God with all your being and to love your neighbor as yourself.

———o———

# QUESTIONS TO DISCUSS

**1.** Why do we find it easier to express our love to another human being rather than being fully devoted to the Lord in abandoned love?

_____

_____

_____

_____

_____

**2.** What are some ways in which you can express or demonstrate your wholehearted love for God, as you love Him with all your heart and soul?

_____

_____

_____

_____

_____

**3.** What are some ways in which we can love the Lord with our mind? How can we improve the sanctity of our thought lives?

_____

_____

_____

_____

_____

**4.** What does it mean to love the Lord with all our strength? How do you know whether you are doing that?

_____

_____

_____

_____

_____

**5.** If your love for the Lord had a gauge or meter, what would be its reading? What is the simplest way to learn to love God more?

_____

_____

_____

_____

_____

*"In the Bible, the 'heart' is more than a pumping station. It is the command center of the body, where decisions are made and plans are hatched. It is the center of our inner being, which controls our feelings, emotions, desires, and passions."*[12]

~ David E. Garland

# Conclusion
## *Questions God Is Asking*

———o———

AS LONG AS YOU'RE ALIVE, YOU'LL HAVE QUESTIONS.
Some arise from a curious mind; others from an anxious
heart. I hope this book has provided some helpful answers,
and I pray you've seen the wisdom of taking all your
questions to the Lord and searching His Word for wisdom
from above. Personally, I have a few questions that may
remain unanswered until heaven, but I've never had a cry
in my heart or mind that didn't find comfort in the truth of
God's Word.

What a remarkable book is the Bible! Though timeless,
it's timely. It's without error, but it shows us our errors
and helps us correct them. It reveals to us the holiness of
God, the mercy of Christ, the power of Calvary, the way to
heaven, and the life that wins. It contains all the answers we
need even when we don't always understand the questions.
It's the only book in the world with an Author constantly

available to answer our questions and give us insight as we prayerfully study its pages.

But now in these closing paragraphs, I'd like to flip the subject around. What if the title of this book had been *Questions God Is Asking?* What would have been the chapter headings? If Almighty God were to speak audibly to you right now, what would He want to know? What questions would He ask?

Here again we can turn to Scripture where we find some probing questions directed our way by the heart of God and from the lips of Jesus. I've selected four to share with you on these final pages.

- *What do you think about the Christ?* Jesus asked this question of the Pharisees in Matthew 22:42. It's the most important question in the world. Who is Jesus Christ? And who is He to you? Our earthly happiness and eternal destiny depend on how we answer that question. The Bible teaches that Jesus Christ is God Himself who became a man—"now in flesh appearing"—who offered Himself as an innocent sacrifice for our sins. His death on the cross and resurrection from the tomb are essential to being reconciled with God. This is grace—not that we loved God but that He loved us and sent His Son, Jesus Christ, to save us from our sins.

- *For what will it profit a man if he gains the whole world and loses his own soul?* Those words in Mark 8:36 also come from Jesus as He spoke of the cost of following Him. When we become Jesus-followers, there is a cost involved. Jesus gave His life for us, but we must also give our lives to Him. "Whoever desires to come after Me, let him deny himself, and take up his cross and follow Me," Jesus said in verse 34. But, lest we think that's too high a cost, He reminded us of the alternative in verse 36: What good is gaining the whole world if, in the process, we lose our own souls? How would you answer Him?

- *How shall we escape if we neglect so great a salvation?* This question comes from Hebrews 2:3, warning us that even after we have some idea about who Christ is and about the importance of following Him, we can put off our decision. We can procrastinate and wait for a more convenient time. We can neglect Him. But nothing is more dangerous than gambling with our soul. The Bible says, "Behold, now is the accepted time; behold, now is the day of salvation" (2 Corinthians 6:2).

- *Do you understand what I have done for you?* Jesus asked this question of His disciples in the Upper Room in John 13:12. He wanted them to know how much He loved them and what a great price He was paying for their eternal welfare. When we get a glimpse of His love and grace for us, we want to receive it, embrace it, rejoice in it, and walk in the light of His love every day.

David Henderson, in his book *Culture Shift*, wrote, "Our lives, like our Daytimers, are busy, busy, busy, full of things to do, places to go, and people to see. Many of us, convinced that the opposite of an empty life is a full schedule, remain content to press on and ignore the deeper questions."[1]

Take a moment now to slow down for a few moments and consider the deeper questions, the questions God is asking of you. Perhaps something in this book has given you a glimpse of His love for you in sending Jesus Christ as His gift from heaven to you. Perhaps you're ready to receive Him as your Lord and Savior. You don't have to neglect Him for another day. Right where you are—at home, on an airplane, in a coffee shop—you can bow your head in prayer and sincerely ask God to forgive all your sins and to help you to turn from them. You can invite Him into your life and profess Him as both Savior and Lord. You can make a definite lifelong decision to become a child of God. You can begin living for Him starting now, developing a life of prayer and Bible study, finding new friends at a Bible-teaching church, and sharing your newfound faith with others.

I pray that you'll do that before you close the covers of this book. Jesus not only answers the questions of your heart. He Himself *is* the answer. He is the light of the world. He is the way, the truth, and the life.

———◇———

# Notes

———o———

## INTRODUCTION

1. Quoted by Lou Cannon, "'Reaganisms' of the Year," *The Philadelphia Inquirer*, January 3, 1989, http://articles.philly.com/1989-01-03/ news/26121743_1_larry-speakes-economic-summit-reagan-and-soviet-leader. Widely quoted in other media outlets.

2. Mark 10:51; Matthew 16:13; Matthew 16:15; Matthew 12:48; Matthew 9:4; John 21:15; Luke 8:45; Mark 8:36; Luke 12:24; Luke 12:26; John 20:15; Mark 6:38; Luke 17:17; Matthew 9:28; Mark 5:39; Luke 6:46; John 13:38; Matthew 26:40; Luke 24:17; John 18:11; Matthew 27:46.

3. Quoted by Robert Christy, *Proverbs, Maxims, and Phrases of All Ages* (New York: G. P. Putnam's Sons, 1887), 184.

## CHAPTER 1  HOW CAN I BE SURE OF MY SALVATION?

1. John Huffman, "Who Are You, and Where Are You Going?" Preaching Conference, 2002.

2. Bill Bright, *How to Be Sure You Are a Christian* (Campus Crusade for Christ, 1972), 5.

3. Tony Evans, *Totally Saved* (Chicago: Moody Press, 2002), 145.

4. Donald Whitney, *How Can I Be Sure I'm a Christian?* (Colorado Springs, CO: NavPress Publishing Group, 1994), 14.

5. Steven J. Lawson, *Absolutely Sure* (Sisters, OR: Multnomah Publishers, 1999), 22.

6. Ibid., 19.

7. Ford C. Ottman, *J. Wilbur Chapman: A Biography* (Garden City, NY: Doubleday, Page & Company, 1920), 29-30.

8. Robert J. Morgan, *Simple: The Christian Life Doesn't Have to be Complicated* (Nashville: Randall House Publications, 2006), 3.

9. Carl F. H. Henry, *The Pacific Garden Mission* (Grand Rapids: Zondervan, 1942), 80-82.

10. Dan R. Ebener, *Servant Leadership Models for Your Parish* (Mahwah, NJ: Paulist Press, 2010), 36.

11. 1 John 2:10; 3:1, 11, 14, 16-18, 23; 4:7-8, 10, 12.

12. Max Lucado, *In the Grip of Grace* (Nashville: Nelson, 1996), 70, quoted in Brady Boyd, *Sons and Daughters* (Grand Rapids: Zondervan, 2012), 40.

**CHAPTER 2 HOW CAN I OVERCOME TEMPTATION?**

1. John White, *The Fight* (Downers Grove, IL: InterVarsity, 1976), 78.

2. David M. Ciocchi, "Understanding Our Ability to Endure Temptation: A Theological Watershed," *JETS*, Volume 35, no. 4 (1992): 463-479.

3. Russell D. Moore, *Tempted and Tried* (Wheaton, IL: Crossway, 2011), 20, 22.

4. Quoted by William H. White, *The Autobiography of Mark Rutherford* (London: Trubner & Co., 1889), 311.

5. Bryan Chapell, *Holiness by Grace* (Wheaton, IL: Crossway, 2001), 102-103.

6. Personal interview with Robert J. Morgan.

7. R. A. Torrey, *How to Succeed in the Christian Life* (New York: Fleming H. Revell Company, 1906), 76.

8. Mark Twain, *The Writings of Mark Twain: Following the Equator* (New York: Harper & Brothers Publishing, 1899), 339.

9. http://www.christianquotes.info/quotes-by-topic/quotes-about-temptation.

10. David Martyn Lloyd-Jones, *Studies in the Sermon on the Mount* (Grand Rapids: Wm. B. Eerdmans Publishing, 1971), 76-77.

11. Erwin Lutzer, "Those Sins that Won't Budge," *Moody Magazine*, March 1978, 48.

12. J. Oswald Sanders, *A Spiritual Clinic* (Chicago: Moody Press, 1961), 20.

13. Vance Havner, *Pleasant Paths* (Grand Rapids: Baker Book House, 1945), 72.

14. David Hegg, *The Obedience Option* (Christian Focus Publications, 2011), 27-28.

15. Quoted in *Holy Thoughts on Holy Things*, selected and arranged by E. Davies (London: Ward, Lock, & Co., n.d.), 578.

### CHAPTER 3    HOW CAN I GET VICTORY OVER WORRY?

1. Scott Stossel, "Surviving Anxiety," *The Atlantic*, December 22, 2013, http://www.theatlantic.com/magazine/archive/2014/01/surviving _anxiety/355741/.

2. Attributed to Elizabeth Cheney, 1859.

3. Ron Dunn, Lifestyle Ministries.

4. C. H. Spurgeon, *Spurgeon's Popular Exposition of Matthew* (London: Marshall, Morgan, and Scott, 1962), 39.

5. J. Hudson Taylor, *Hudson Taylor's Choice Sayings: A Compilation from His Writings and Addresses* (London: China Inland Mission, n.d.), 52.

6. Adapted from Richard S. Greene, "Where Will the Money Come From?" in *Decision Magazine*, May 1997, 32-33.

7. John R. W. Stott, *The Message of The Sermon on the Mount* (Downers Grove, IL: InterVarsity Press, 1978), 168.

8. This is a commonly seen sermon illustration. See, for example, "For Fretters and Worriers Only" by Lester J. Harnish, *Eternity Magazine*, Vol. 15, no. 10, October 1964, 21.

9. Dale Carnegie, *How to Stop Worrying and Start Living* (New York: Simon and Schuster, 1948), 6, 10.

10. Ray Johnston, *The Hope Quotient: Measure It. Raise It. You'll Never Be the Same* (Nashville: Thomas Nelson, Inc., 2014), 133.

11. Generic illustration; original source unknown.


### CHAPTER 4    HOW CAN I FIND FORGIVENESS?

1. Max Lucado, *In the Grip of Grace* (Nashville: Thomas Nelson, Inc., 1996), 149-150.

2. Donald Williams, *The Preacher's Commentary: Psalms 1-72* (Nashville: Thomas Nelson, Inc., 1986), Kindle edition.

3. "Hayman Fire Starter Praying for Forgiveness," *Associated Press*, July 5, 2004, www.thedenverchannel.com.

4. Michael Vick, "Michael Vick: I Blame Me," *CBS News*, August 10, 2009, http://www.cbsnews.com/news/michael-vick-i-blame-me/.

5. S. Trevor Francis, "O the Deep, Deep Love of Jesus," 1875.

6. Tremper Longman III & David E. Garland, *The Expositor's Bible Commentary: Psalms* (Grand Rapids: Zondervan, 2008), 312.

7. Rosalind Goforth, *Climbing* (Wheaton, IL: Sword Book Club, 1940), 90.

8. Stuart Briscoe, *The One Year Book of Devotions for Men* (Wheaton, IL: Tyndale House Publishers, Inc., 2000), entry for Feb 5.

9. Elmer Towns, *Fasting for Spiritual Breakthrough* (Ventura, CA: Regal, 1996), 37.

10. From the hymn, "How Great Thou Art" by Stuart K. Hine, copyright 1949 and 1953 by the Stuart Hine Trust.

11. Ruby Scott, *Jungle Harvest* (Conservative Baptist Home Mission Society, 1988), 75-80.

12. William Cowper in his hymn, "There is a Fountain Filled With Blood," 1772.

13. Corrie ten Boom, *Each New Day* (Minneapolis, MN: Revell, 1977), devotion for March 21.

## CHAPTER 5   IS THERE ONLY ONE WAY TO GOD?

1. www.leestrobel.com/Bio.php.

2. Lee Strobel, *The Case for Faith Student Edition* (Zondervan: Youth Specialties, 2002), 51-52.

3. Lee Strobel, *The Case for Christ* (Grand Rapids: Zondervan, 2000), 145-146.

4. www.huffingtonpost.com/steve-mcswain/jesus-the-original-new-ag_b_6301140.html.

5. Quoted by LaTonya Taylor, "The Church of O," *Christianity Today*, April 1, 2002, 38.

6. CNN's *Larry King Live*, January 12, 2000.

7. Strobel, *The Case for Faith Student Edition*.

8. I'm indebted to John Phillips for this simple outline, found in his *100 New Testament Sermon Outlines* (Grand Rapids: Kregel Publications, 1979), outline #34.

9. Steven James, *How to Smell Like God* (Cincinnati: Standard Publishing, 2005), 59.

10. John Phillips, *Exploring the Gospel of John* (Grand Rapids: Kregel Publications, 1989), 267.

11. Dave Hunt, *In Defense of the Faith* (Harvest House Publishers, 1996).

12. Quoted in *750 Engaging Illustrations for Preachers, Teachers, and Writers*, edited by Craig Brian Larson (Grand Rapids: Baker Books, 1993), 594.

13. Quoted in *The Case for Faith* by Lee Strobel (Grand Rapids: Zondervan Publishing House, 2000), 166.

14. Austin Gentry, *Gospel Focus 289*, "Most Exclusive and Most Inclusive," September 29, 2013, http://gospelfocus289.wordpress.com/2013/09/29/most-exclusive-most-inclusive/.

15. Bruce Milne, *The Message of John* (Downers Grove, IL: InterVarsity Press, 1993), 212.

16. N. T. Wright, *John for Everyone* (Louisville: Westminster John Knox Press, 2004), 60.

17. John Phillips, *Exploring the Gospel of John* (Grand Rapids: Kregel Publications, 1989), 265.

**CHAPTER 6 WHY DO CHRISTIANS HAVE SO MANY PROBLEMS?**

1. Howard Rutledge, *In the Presence of Mine Enemies* (Old Tappan, NJ: Revell, 1973), 24-26.

2. John Maxwell, *Your Attitude: Key to Success* (San Bernardino, CA: Here's Life Publishers, 1984), 99.

3. Isobel Kuhn, *In the Arena* (Singapore: OMF International, 1995), vii-viii.

4. William Secker, *The Nonsuch Professor* (Chicago: Fleming H. Revell Company, 1899), 77.

5. Ibid., 22.

6. John Faris, *Old Roads Out of Philadelphia* (Philadelphia: J.B. Lippincott, 1917), 137.

7. *Turning Points Magazine*, September 2012, daily devotion for September 6.

8. Kay Arthur, "My Disappointments, His Appointments," in *Moody Magazine*, January 1992, 30.

9. W. H. Griffith Thomas, *Genesis, A Devotional Commentary* (Grand Rapids: Eerdmans Publishing, 1946), 376.

10. Tim Keller, *Walking with God Through Pain and Suffering* (NY: Penguin Group, 2013), 5.

11. Hebrews 2:17-18 and 4:15.

12. Tullian Tchividjian, *Glorious Ruin: How Suffering Sets You Free* (Colorado Springs: David C. Cook, 2012), Kindle edition.

13. Robert J. Morgan, *The Promise* (Nashville: B&H Publishers, 2008), 143.

14. Rutledge, *In the Presence of Mine Enemies*, 8-9.

15. Ibid., 29-30.

16. Ibid., 62-64.

17. Ibid., 90.

18. *The Banner of Truth Magazine*, published in Hackensack, New Jersey, July 1, 1871, Vol. VI, no. 1, 3.


CHAPTER 7 WHY DON'T MY PRAYERS GET ANSWERED?

1. John Loveland, *Blessed Assurance: The Life and Hymns of Fanny J. Crosby* (Nashville: Broadman Press, 1978), 22.

2. *Fanny Crosby Speaks Again*, ed. by Dr. Donald P. Hustad (Carol Stream, IL: Hope Publishing Co., 1977), 93.

3. J. Oswald Sanders, *Prayer Power Unlimited* (Chicago: Moody Press, 1977), 87-88.

4. Cameron V. Thompson, *Master Secrets of Prayer* (Madison, GA: Light for Living Publications, 1990), 38.

5. The results of this survey were widely reported, including at http://www.examiner.com/article/how-americans-spend-their-time-american-time-use-survey-by-u-s-labor-dept.

6. Virginia Law, *Appointment Congo* (Chicago: Rand McNally & Co., 1966), 20-21.

7. Quoted at http://www.calvarychapel.com/redbarn/pquotes.htm, accessed May 21, 2005.

8. Rick Hampson, "Can You Forgive?" *USA Today*, January 18, 2013, 1A.

9. *Turning Points Magazine*, September 2011, devotional thought for September 24/25.

10. Mike Fleischmann, *Discipleship Journal*, "Prayer Blockers," Issue 97: Jan./Feb. 1997.

11. Bill Hybels, *Too Busy Not To Pray* (Downers Grove, IL: InterVarsity Press, 1988), 74.

12. David Jeremiah, *Prayer: The Great Adventure* (Sisters, OR: Multnomah Publishers, Inc., 1997), 69-70.

13. Quoted by Charlie Jones and Bob Kelly in *The Tremendous Power of Prayer* (West Monroe, LA: Howard Publishing Co., 2000), 53.


CHAPTER 8 IS THERE A SIN GOD CANNOT FORGIVE?

1. Billy Graham, *The Holy Spirit* (Nashville: Thomas Nelson, 1988), 154.

2. William Cowper, *Memoir of the Early Life of William Cowper, Esq* (London: R. Edwards, 1818), 68-69.

3. John Bunyan, *The Life of John Bunyan* (London: Samuel Bagster and Sons, 1845), 24.

4. Charles Grandison Finney, *Memoirs of Rev. Charles G. Finney* (New York: A. S. Barnes & Company, 1876), 18.

5. https://www.bradpaisley.com/music/songs/those-crazy-christians.

6. parade.com/4188/erinhill/brad-paisley-tackles-religion-in-that-other-controversial-song-those-crazy-christians/.

7. Mike Barrett, "Searching for Radical Faith," *Christianity Today*, February 27, 2009, http://www.christianitytoday.com/ct/2009/february/30.36.html?paging=off.

8. Kay Arthur, *As Silver Refined: Learning to Embrace Life's Disappointments* (Colorado Springs: Waterbrook Press, 1997), 239.

9. Alfred Plummer, *An Exegetical Commentary on the Gospel According to St. Matthew* (London: Scott, 1909), 179.

10. John MacArthur, *The Jesus You Can't Ignore* (Nashville: Thomas Nelson, 2008), 175.

11. B. H. Carroll (Pastor, Theologian, Teacher, Author), Southwest Baptist Theological Seminary (Fort Worth, TX).

12. Hank Hanegraaff, *The Bible Answer Book, Volume 2* (Nashville: Thomas Nelson, 2006), 67.

### CHAPTER 9   WHAT IS FAITH?

1. Sheila Walsh, *Beautiful Things Happen When a Woman Trusts God* (Nashville: Thomas Nelson, 2010), ix.

2. Ron Dunn, *The Faith Crisis* (Wheaton, IL: Tyndale House, 1984), 19-21.

3. John MacArthur, *The Gospel According to the Apostles* (Nashville: Thomas Nelson, 2000), 25.

4. Adapted from "Living With Confidence—a Sermon from Hebrews 11" by Robert J. Morgan.

5. Ibid.

6. John Phillips, *Exploring Hebrews* (Grand Rapids: Kregel Publications, 2002), 149.

7. *The Oswald Chambers Devotional Reader*, edited by Harry Verploegh (Nashville: Thomas Nelson, 1990), 76.

8. Katie J. Davis, *Kisses from Katie* (New York: Howard Books, 2011), 107.

9. J. Gresham Machen, *What Is Faith?* (Edinburgh: Banner of Truth, 1991), 242.

10. Adapted from John Polkinghorne and Nicholas Beale, *Questions of Truth* (Westminster John Knox Press, 2009), 26-27.

11. MacArthur, *The Gospel According to the Apostles*, 27.

12. John Bisagno, *The Power of Positive Praying* (Grand Rapids: Zondervan, 1965), 24.

13. Isaac Watts, quoted in *Forty Thousand Sublime and Beautiful Thoughts*, (New York: The Christian Herald Bible House, 1904), 835.

14. Luci Swindoll, *Doing Life Differently* (Nashville: Thomas Nelson, 2010), 256-257.

15. B. B. McKinney, "Have Faith in God," *Baptist Hymnal* (Nashville: Lifeway Worship, 2008), #508.

16. *Matthew Henry's Concise Commentary on the Whole Bible* (Nashville: Thomas Nelson, 1997), 1214.

**CHAPTER 10 WHAT IS THE GREATEST COMMANDMENT?**

1. www.surfertoday.com/surfing/11150-surfing-legend-dorian-doc-paskowitz-dies-at-93.

2. "Taylor Swift Confesses She Doesn't 'Fit In,'" http://hollywoodlife.com/2014/08/27/taylor-swift-video-outtakes-shake-it-off/, accessed September 10, 2014.

3. www.huffingtonpost.com/amanda-gore/the-one-thing_2_b_5279013.html.

4. www.brainyquote.com/quotes/keywords/the_most_important.html.

5. www.thebestnotes.com/booknotes/Tuesdays_With_Morrie_Albom/Tuesdays_With_Morrie_Study_Guide17.html.

6. "Paulo Coelho Explains Why Courage Is The Most Important Spiritual Quality," September 9, 2014, www.huffingtonpost.com/2014/09/09/paulo-coelho-alchemist-spiritual-people_n_5786482.html?utm_hp_ref=own&ir=OWN, accessed September 10, 2014.

7. Widely quoted, including by Bud Greenspan in *100 Greatest Moments in Olympic History* (General Pub. Group, 1995), 223.

8. www.goodreads.com/author/show/298322.Helen_Roseveare.

9. James Emery White, *A Mind for God* (Downers Grove, IL: InterVarsity Press, 2006), 15.

10. Gene Edward Veith, Jr., *Loving God with All Your Mind* (Wheaton, IL: Crossway Books, 2003), 150.

# NOTES

11. Linda's story is told in *Everyday Heroes: True Stories of Faith, Hope, and Compassion* (Cleveland, TN: Life Care Centers of America, 2003), 2-3.

12. David E. Garland, *The NIV Application Commentary: Mark* (Grand Rapids, MI: Zondervan, 1996), Kindle edition.

## CONCLUSION

1. David W. Henderson, *Culture Shift: Communicating God's Truth to Our Changing World* (Grand Rapids: Baker House Books, 1998).

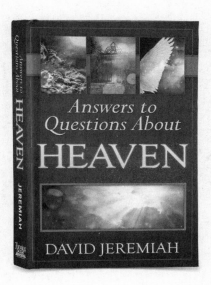

## *Answers to Questions About Heaven*

When it comes down to it, people have questions about heaven—and the Bible has answers. In fact, this topic is mentioned more than 500 times in the Bible so that we might envision the place God is preparing for His children. In this question-and-answer guide, Dr. Jeremiah answers your questions, including "Is heaven a real, physical place?" and "What kinds of rewards will believers receive in heaven?" These questions and more will build our understanding and whet our appetite for heaven.

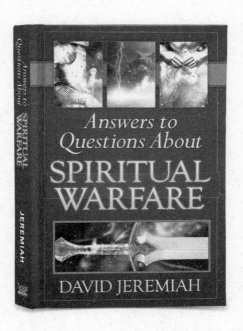

## *Answers to Questions About Spiritual Warfare*

Troubling circumstances have a way of claiming our attention and often leave us implementing ineffective strategies to overcome them. But the Bible says God has ultimate victory. He has given each of us the tools to be victorious over our own spiritual warfare. In this guide, Dr. Jeremiah provides godly, biblical answers to the questions we have about spiritual warfare, like "How can I discern Satan's lies from truth?" and "What armor has God given me for warfare?" Learn how to be victorious over the enemy using the tools God has provided for us with *Answers to Questions About Spiritual Warfare*.

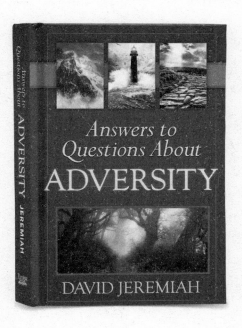

## Answers to Questions
## About Adversity

With each new day come new trials. Adversity is no walk in the park and often makes us wonder, Why is life so hard? The Bible has answers for us filled with rich, grace-filled truths. In this question-and-answer guide, Dr. Jeremiah uses a lifetime of studying biblical doctrine to answer some of our toughest questions, including "How do I keep my family from falling apart?" and "Does God give second chances?" This book offers encouraging truths from the Word on how to walk in faith—trusting the One who defeated the Adversary to be your hope and comfort in trials as well.